THE FIRST SOCIALIST REPUBLIC, THE SOVIET UNION

THE FIRST SOCIALIST REPUBLIC, *THE SOVIET UNION*

Gerald McIsaac

ISBN: 978-1-957009-01-8 (hc)
ISBN: 978-1-957009-00-1 (sc)
ISBN: 978-1-952302-99-2 (e)

Library of Congress Control Number: 2021924330

TABLE OF CONTENTS

PREFACE

The revolutionary motion is currently gripping the country. Countless working people, those who were formerly apathetic, are now being swept up in the movement, taking an interest in politics.

Remarkably enough, this is to be expected. As Lenin phrased it, "symptomatic of any genuine revolution is a rapid, tenfold and even hundredfold increase in the size of the working and oppressed masses—hitherto apathetic-who are capable of waging the political struggle." That which we are now experiencing is a" genuine revolution".

Most of the people who are rising up, taking part in the revolution, are not aware of that which they are doing. The reason for this is quite simple. They are not class conscious. The conditions of life of the working class, the proletariat, do not lead to the awareness of themselves as a class. That awareness must come from an outside source, and that outside source is middle class intellectuals. Bear in mind that both Marx and Lenin were such middle-class intellectuals. I mention this for the benefit of those who are prejudiced against the middle class.

There is currently no shortage of middle-class intellectuals in the working class, or more accurately former members of the middle class, technically referred to as the petty bourgeois. The current crisis in capitalism has ruined a great many members of that class, forcing them into bankruptcy and the ranks of the proletariat. They bring with them their knowledge of classes, and of the revolutionary theories of Marx and Lenin. Welcome, fellow intellectuals! Now is the time to put that knowledge to good work!

This is another way of saying that they should come together and take part in the formation of a truly Communist Party, which is to say one that advocates for the Dictatorship Of the Proletariat. All other parties which claim to be Communist, but deny the necessity of that Dictatorship, are merely social chauvinists, socialists in words, chauvinists in deeds. They are among the most loyal, devoted servants of the capitalists, and should be treated as such.

Such parties are not to be confused with the utopian socialists, those who consider socialism to be a fine idea. Such people may or may not be members of a party. Some of them are members of groups or organizations, and as such, tend to fight for democracy and socialism, or even mere reforms. These people are our friends, the natural and desirable allies of the working class. They are not the enemy!

The capitalists, the super-rich, the billionaires, technically referred to as the bourgeoisie, are well aware of that which is happening. They know that a revolution is "right around the corner", and are determined to stop it, or at least divert it onto some harmless path of social reform. By way of contrast with the working class, technically called the proletariat, the capitalists are well aware of themselves as a class. They hold state power, and fully intend to maintain that power. They are also well aware of the revolutionary theories of Marx and Lenin. For that reason, they consider the followers of Marx and Lenin, Communists, to be their most dangerous enemies. In this, they are correct.

The capitalists are also well aware that the one and only alternative to capitalism, is socialism. For that reason, they are making a supreme effort to slander the leaders of the first socialist republic. Of course, I am referring to Lenin and Stalin, the leaders of the Soviet Union.

The focus of this article is on the newly awakened members of the working class, those who have just recently become politically active. It is only natural that such people should be confused, as all have been bombarded with capitalist propaganda, all their lives. The lies and deception of the capitalists, the bourgeois, is intense and effective. It must be countered.

This article is written in a popular manner, but with a few technical terms. This is necessary, as working people have to learn such terms. The lack of awareness of the working people, of such terms, is frequently used against them. Also, a certain amount of repetition is deliberate, as we all learn through repetition.

The book concerns the first socialist republic, the Soviet Union, and the two great revolutionary leaders, Lenin and Stalin. It contains twelve parts.

PART 1

THE FIRST RUSSIAN REVOLUTION OF 1917

By 1914, the Romanov family had been ruling the Russian Empire for three centuries. Nicholas the Second, or Nicholas the Bloody, was the Czar, or Emperor, and his power was almost absolute. The Empire was vast, several times bigger than the United States, and various countries were subjugated, within the Empire.

Then in August of 1914, the Russian Empire joined an alliance with the countries of Great Britain, France, Italy, Romania and Japan, referred to as the Allied Powers, or the Entente. Those countries then went to war with the Central Powers, that of Germany, Austria-Hungary, Bulgaria and the Ottoman Empire, also known as the Quadruple Alliance. It should be noted that the Ottoman Empire was essentially the country known today as Turkey. There followed the great slaughter, which became known as the First World War.

At that time, the world had been divided up between the "great powers", which is to say the most highly developed capitalist countries, especially Great Britain, France, America and Germany. In those countries, at or around the turn of the century, capitalism had reached the stage of monopoly, otherwise known as imperialism. There is nothing progressive about imperialism, and in fact it is complete reaction, to the very core of its being. The capitalists of those countries, which is to say the imperialists, were interested only in world financial supremacy. With that in mind, their focus was on plundering and strangling foreign countries. Yet they were squabbling among themselves, as is characteristic of capitalists, especially as Germany wanted more colonies.

As the world was already divided up between the imperialist powers, this meant that the only way Germany could get more colonies was by stealing them from the other imperialist countries. This was only possible through war. To that end, the imperialists of Germany formed an alliance with the imperialists of several other countries, in an attempt to get a more "equitable" share of the world. Of course, the imperialists of the opposing countries took a "dim view" of these proceedings. Hence the First World War.

In 1914, Russia was one of the more "backward" countries, to use the vernacular of the time. By this is meant that most of her people were peasants, three quarters in fact, and almost all of those peasants were completely illiterate. But at the same time, she had a rather impressive population of possibly one hundred sixty million people. The capitalists of Great Britain and France considered this to be a valuable source of "cannon fodder". This is to say that the Russian soldiers were regarded as valuable material, to be expended in war. In other words, to be sacrificed.

This war led to a split within the ranks of the Social Democrats, as the Marxists of the time referred to themselves. (It was only later that they became known as Communists.) The true Marxists became known as Bolsheviks, and opposed the war, while the social chauvinists, who were referred to as Mensheviks, called for "defence of the fatherland". In this way, the social chauvinists showed their "true colours".

The Russian Bolsheviks, led by Lenin, did their best to transform the slaughter of working people, by working people, into a civil war, workers against capitalists. As Lenin was in exile at the time, in Switzerland, it was exceptionally difficult. For that matter, most of the Bolsheviks were also either in prison or exiled.

Yet the revolutionary motion of the Russian common people, by which I mean the workers and peasants, carried on and even intensified. The war did not sidetrack the revolution. It intensified the revolution. By that time, the Russian working people were veterans, as most had first experienced revolution in 1905. Not that the revolution of 1905 had succeeded in overthrowing the Czar, but it had succeeded in training vast numbers of revolutionary fighters.

The situation is similar to that which we have today in America, in that a great many people are active, seasoned veterans of the occupy movement of several years ago. Those same people are now taking part in the Autonomous Zone movement of today. They have no illusions. They know what to expect.

To return to Russia of 1917, Lenin pointed out that the "Great War", as it was then called, did not stop the revolutionary movement. On the contrary, this war served as a "stage manager", one which was capable of "vastly accelerating the course of world history, and on the other, of engendering world wide crises of unparalleled intensity—economic, political, national and international."

The astute reader may find this to be an accurate description of the current situation! The twin crises of the Corona Virus and the Depression has served to intensify the world wide revolutionary motion.

In America, the capitalists are proudly proclaiming that "merely" a few hundred citizens are dying each day, as a result of the virus. In other parts of the world, such as India, the medical system has broken down. The medical staff has been working to the point of exhaustion, they have run out of beds, out of oxygen and other medical supplies. People who are desperately sick are being turned away. It is possible that the virus has mutated, to a more toxic strain. That more toxic strain could spread to the rest of the world, and the medical situation in India could soon be seen in America.

Yet the capitalists have their priorities well established. Those who are not moving, are not spending money. Those who are not spending money, are not creating a profit for the capitalists. For that reason, "travel restrictions" are being "lifted". Ever more people are being allowed, even encouraged, to move around and spend their money. At the same time, they are bound to spread the virus. God help us if the virus mutates!

Under similar circumstances, in Russia, 1917, the common people, which is to say the workers and peasants, rose up in revolution. The movement was "for *bread*, for *peace,* for *real freedom.*" (italics by Lenin) To the astonishment of almost the whole world, the Romanov's, those whom had been ruling the Russian Empire for three centuries, were overthrown, during the eight days of February-March, 1917.

Not that the common people, the workers and peasants, accomplished this incredible feat alone. By no means. They had help. That help came from an extremely unlikely source. Perhaps it is best to let Lenin explain the events that led up to this revolution:

"That the revolution succeeded so quickly and—seemingly, at the first superficial glance—so radically, is only due to the fact that, as a result of an extremely unique historical situation, *absolutely dissimilar currents, absolutely heterogenous* class interests, *absolutely contrary* political and social strivings have *merged,* and in a strikingly 'harmonious' manner. Namely, the conspiracy of the Anglo-French imperialists, who impelled Milyukov, Guchkov and Co. to seize power *for the purpose of continuing the imperialist war,* for the purpose of conducting the war still more ferociously and obstinately, for the purpose of *slaughtering fresh millions* of Russian workers and peasants . . . This on the one hand. On the other, there was a profound proletarian and mass popular movement of a revolutionary character (a movement of the entire poorest section of the population of town and country) for *bread,* for *peace,* for *real freedom.*" (italics by Lenin)

Of course, the people of Russia knew precisely that to which Lenin was referring. Yet, modern day Americans may not be so well informed. So with that in mind, allow me to clarify the situation.

The capitalist leaders, the imperialists, of Britain and France, were not at all happy with the manner in which Czar Nicholas was "prosecuting the war". They were of the opinion that he was not terribly enthusiastic, at least when it came to sending countless Russian soldiers to their death, attacking fortified enemy positions. Worse, there was a "vicious rumour" circulating to the effect that Russia was negotiating a "separate peace" with Germany. Of course, the Russian diplomats denied this, but the British and French did not believe them. After all, the Russian capitalists are highly skilled liars, as are the capitalists of Britain and France.

So in the interest of "*slaughtering fresh millions* of Russian workers and peasants", they decided to "meddle in Russian politics", in order to have the Czar overthrown, and replaced by "moderates". It was expected that these people would be more "sweetly reasonable", that they would prosecute the war with greater enthusiasm.

This "palace coup" was not as difficult as it may sound. Both the British and the French had embassies in Saint Petersburg, the capital of Russia. They then used their vast reserves of capitol, their money, to "persuade" the "patriots" of Russia, that it was in the best interest of the country, to overthrow the Czar. In other words, the top Russian officials were bribed.

It is note worthy that it never occurred to the imperialists of either Britain or France, to mind their own business. They did not hesitate to meddle in the internal affairs of another country. That is as true today, as it was in 1917.

This "conspiracy of the Anglo-French imperialists", to overthrow the Czar, in the interests of "*continuing the imperialist war . . .* for the purpose of *slaughtering fresh millions* of Russian workers and peasants", coincided with "a profound proletarian and mass popular movement . . . for *bread,* for *peace,* for *real freedom.*"

To think that the immediate goals of the British and French imperialists were identical to the immediate goals of the working people of Russia! Incredible but true. This is indeed an "extremely unique historical situation". The working people wanted Czar Nicholas gone, in the interests of peace, while the British and French imperialists wanted him gone, but in the interests of war! Lenin refers to this as "*absolutely contrary* political and social strivings have *merged*", which resulted in the abdication of Czar Nicholas.

There is a lesson in all this. There are times, especially when the class struggle reaches the point of open rebellion, that the immediate goals of one class are precisely the same as the goals of another class. This is true, even when the two classes are the bitterest of enemies. Of course, as soon as the immediate goals are reached, the alliance is immediately ended. At that point, the two classes return to the serious business of destroying each other.

As an example, to which most Americans can relate, this happened in America, in early 1861. At that time, the country was falling apart. The two principle warring classes were composed of the southern slave owners, those who were completely reactionary, and determined to block any industrial development. The second class was the capitalists, who were equally determined to invest their capitol in the southern regions.

This took place before capitalism reached the stage of monopoly, which is of course imperialism, so that the capitalists had certain progressive features. Their single minded determination to destroy the slave owners was most commendable, even if their motives were less than honourable. Their one and only concern was with their profit, so that they cared about as much about the slaves, as they cared about their own wage slaves, their workers. In other words, not in the slightest.

With that in mind, in the interests of destroying the slave owners, the northern capitalists *formed an alliance with the slave owners!* Incredible but true.

As for those who are skeptical, bear in mind that the southern slave states broke away, and formed a Confederacy. They immediately designed their own flag, the "stars and bars". Each star represents one state. Yet even though eleven states separated, the Confederate rag proudly displays thirteen stars. The two surplus stars represent the states of Missouri and Kentucky. Those two states came that close to separating!

At the "last minute", the northern capitalists decided to engage in a little "damage control", as the state of Missouri was famous for their mules, and the state of Kentucky was famous for their long rifles. The capitalists were anxious to employ both in the forthcoming war effort. With that in mind, they quickly assured the slave owners of those two states, as well as the slave owners of Delaware, Maryland and West Virginia, the five so called "border states", that they could keep their slaves, as long as they agreed to wage war with the "breakaway states". Those particular slave owners agreed, and promptly took part in ensuring their own destruction.

The conscious acts of the American capitalists, in 1861, stands in stark contrast to the actions of the workers and peasants of Russia, in early 1917. They rose up spontaneously, and managed to overthrow the Czar. They had no way of knowing that they were assisted in this noble endeavour by the imperialists of Britain and France. They just knew that they were cold, hungry, crushed and being slaughtered by Germany and her friends. Most of the Russian soldiers were peasants, and they wanted land to call their own. As well, they all wanted peace and bread, as well as some democratic rights.

In opposition to this were the forces of reaction, which included the nobility, landlords and capitalists. They were all focused on carrying on the war. The landlords were determined to keep their land, at the expense of the peasants, and to place another Romanov on the throne. The capitalists were more practical. They merely wanted more profit.

PART 2

LENIN RETURNS TO RUSSIA

During this time of great upheaval, within Russia, Lenin was living in the country of Switzerland. This was not so much a matter of choice on his part, but a natural result of being exiled, many years earlier. With the Czar out of the way, he was of course anxious to return to his native country. As he was a Russian citizen, and Russia was at war with Germany, this was not an easy task. The only way to get to Russia was through Germany. Yet, diplomatic channels were opened, and he, as well as possibly thirty other Russian nationals, were placed on a sealed train and allowed to travel through Germany, to Russia. In early April, 1917, Lenin arrived in Saint Petersburg. A great crowd met him at the train station, and gave him a thunderous round of applause. The working people once again had their leader!

The spontaneous revolution of early 1917 had succeeded in overthrowing the Czar, and had allowed the capitalists, the bourgeoisie, to establish a democratic republic. As Lenin pointed out, such a republic is the "best possible political shell for capitalism". Indeed, the common people, the workers and peasants, were granted certain democratic rights, at least on paper. Yet the war continued and the suffering, the cold and hunger of the people continued as before. The working people had gone as far as they could go, on their own. Now it was up to their leaders, the Bolsheviks, led by Lenin, to bring them the class consciousness they needed. Only in that way could they carry the revolution forward to victory, to socialism, to the Dictatorship Of the Proletariat.

Now the working people in various parts of the world are rising up, spontaneously, as there are no proper Communists Parties to lead them. The only true Communist Parties are those which call for the Dictatorship Of the Proletariat. As Lenin stated, that is the "touchstone" of a true Marxist.

In Russia, the working people were well aware that the Czar cared only for himself and his immediate family. The events of Bloody Sunday, in January of 1905, removed all doubt, in that respect. On that day, many thousands of peaceful protesters, loyal subjects of His Majesty, led by a priest with a petition, marched on the Winter Palace of the Czar. The Czar responded by turning loose his Cossacks. Several thousand citizens were either killed or wounded. After Bloody Sunday, the Russian people remained the subjects of His Majesty, just not so loyal. In fact, that served as the spark that ignited the revolution of 1905. It raged for over two years, and failed to dislodge the Czar, but did train countless revolutionaries. The working people of Russia became veterans. They had no illusions.

We are faced with a similar situation now in North America. The Occupy Movement of several years ago, largely failed to achieve its goals. This is not too surprising as there were no Communist leaders. The protesters were not class conscious. People were moving in that direction, in that there was a vague reference to the "one percent". Yet the posters and banners made no reference to classes. Capitalism was never mentioned.

Now the revolutionary motion is once again rising up, and it is even stronger and finer. The American working class still has no Communist Party to lead them, to bring them the awareness of themselves as a class, and of their destiny to overthrow the capitalists, the bourgeoisie, and to establish the Dictatorship Of the Proletariat. Yet they no longer refer to the super rich, the billionaires, the bourgeoisie, as the one percent. As there are only a few hundred billionaires in all of North America, they compose perhaps one in a million, as opposed to one in a hundred. There is no doubt a growing awareness of this fact.

Equally without doubt, an American Communist Party, Dictatorship Of the Proletariat, ACP, DOP. will soon be formed. The capitalists will see to that! Of necessity, such a Party must be created by intellectuals, those who are aware of the revolutionary theories of Marx and Lenin. Most such intellectuals are members of the middle class, the petty bourgeois, and they tend to be well educated. Yet the middle class is being wiped out, financially ruined, driven into bankruptcy and the ranks of the working class, the proletariat. They bring with them their knowledge of the revolutionary theories of Marx and Lenin. These are the people we can count upon to create a new, truly Marxist, Communist Party.

The citizens of Russia, in April of 1917, did not have that problem. They had Lenin and the Bolsheviks, as the Communists were then called, and Lenin was home, back in Russia.

It may come as a surprise to many, to find that the capitalists are also well aware of the revolutionary theories of Marx. In fact they are supremely well aware of those theories, especially that of the Dictatorship Of the Proletariat. They do that theory the supreme honour of never mentioning it. Then again, they never mention the existence of classes. The less the working class, the proletariat, knows of itself as a class, with its own class interests, the better for the capitalists, the bourgeoisie.

The revolutionary situation of Russia, 1917, was a bit more complicated than that of modern day America. The Czar had been forced from the throne, but he still had a great deal of support. He was "down but not out", and the nobility was still a powerful force. In particular, the landlords were passionate monarchists. The middle class, the petty bourgeois, were also quite numerous, and equally powerful. They tended to vacillate between the working class and the capitalist class, depending upon the class which seemed to be winning. The majority of the people were peasants, in fact three quarters of them, but illiterate and incapable of coming together as a class. As all peasants want to own the land they are tilling, as well as the land of their neighbours, they are in effect small time capitalists. That left the working class, the proletariat, the only truly revolutionary class. Yet that was enough.

Of course the capitalists were well aware of this. They recognized Lenin as the threat that he was. So they decided to "take steps", in order to "nip it in the bud". They realized that they could not stop the revolutionary motion, any more than someone can stand on a beach and stop the tide from coming in. Yet they could divert the motion, onto some harmless path of social reform. It was simply a matter of killing Lenin.

Shortly after Lenin returned to the capitol of Saint Petersburg, the Provisional Government, which became known as the Kerensky regime, determined to kill Lenin. At that time, the government represented the capitalists, the landlords and the nobility. They were united in their determination to continue with the war, and to honour the secret treaties between the Czar and the Anglo-French imperialists.

Modern day American Marxist intellectuals would do well to bear this in mind! The American imperialists are just as well aware of the danger of a Communist Party, as were the Russian imperialists of 1917. Just as the Provisional Government was determined to kill Lenin, so too the American government will attempt to kill any leader of the working class, just as they killed Martin Luther King, in 1968. The fact that he was a pacifist, did not spare King.

This is to say that those who choose to do the right thing, to stand on principle, to create a Communist Party, should take all reasonable precautions. Take advantage of the tools available. There is no need to gather in one place. Use the internet. There is something referred to as the "dark net", which, among other things, is a gathering place for pedophiles. That is about the only thing I know about it. But if the perverts can access this, then so can the Marxists.

Lenin took reasonable precautions, in 1917. With the help of Stalin, he was disguised as a peasant and fled to Finland. There he prepared for the proletarian revolution. In that summer, many Marxists were anxious to carry through the revolution, to overthrow the Provisional Government, and establish socialism. Yet Lenin estimated that the movement was not yet strong enough, and advised them to be patient. At the same time, he wrote State and Revolution, in preparation for the Dictatorship Of the Proletariat. That is the work which is most relevant today.

The months between the return of Lenin to Russia, in April, and the "October Revolution", were quite similar to the time in which we live. (It is called the October Revolution as it took place on October 25, old style calendar, or November 7, new style calendar) Having said that, there were notable differences, all to the advantage of the forthcoming revolution. The situation now is much simpler, as the class conflict has been much simplified.

Here in America, the nobility, in the form of the British monarchy, were given their walking papers many years ago, in the First American Revolution of 1776. Then the slave owners were abolished in the Civl War of 1861-1865. Since that time, the peasants, or farmers, as they refer to themselves, have been practically wiped out. The same is true of the middle class, or petty bourgeois. True, there are still the remnants of those classes in existence, the odd family farmer and the occasional small business owner. Yet they are all "living on borrowed time", and they know it.

The monopoly capitalists, the billionaires, the bourgeoisie, do not take kindly to competition. Working through their corporations, monopolies which are becoming ever stronger, ever more complete, the small business owners, the "little guy", is being squeezed out. Any and all competition is simply not tolerated, no matter how insignificant. That includes the corner store, as well as the family farmer.

If nothing else, that simplifies the class struggle. Now it is the working class, the proletariat, against the monopoly capitalist class, the billionaires, the bourgeoisie. That is the good news, to use that old and worn out joke. The bad news it that we are still cursed with the social chauvinists, those who are socialists in words, chauvinists in deeds. They are to be distinguished by the fact that they claim to be Marxists, but deny the necessity for the Dictatorship Of the Proletariat.

On a serious note, we can only repeat that the social chauvinists are not to be confused with the social democrats, those who are fighting for democracy as well as socialism. They do not claim to be Marxists. Such people are the natural and desirable allies of the working class. They are to be treated with the utmost respect and consideration. In due time, we can count on them to see that we are right.

One of the first problems Lenin faced, upon his return to Russia, was that of "dual power", in the shape of Soviets of Workers, as well as Soviets of Soldiers. Bear in mind that Soviet means Council in Russian. Not that the Soviets were the problem. The problem was that they were voluntarily surrendering their power to the Provisional Government!

These Soviets can be compared to the "Autonomous Zones" of America. They are spontaneously popping up across the country, not necessarily in a geographical sense. Working people have learned that to occupy an area merely results in an attack, by an overpowering force. So now they are taking action, enacting reforms, without staking out a zone.

This is truly remarkable, but not unprecedented. Lenin made reference to these zones, or Soviets: "Nowhere is there, nor can there be, a similar institution because you must have one or the other: *either* a bourgeois government with 'plans' for reforms like those just mapped out to us and proposed dozens of times in every country but remaining on paper, *or* the institution to which they are now referring, the new type of 'government' created by the revolution, examples of which can be found only at a time of greatest revolutionary upsurge, as in France, 1792 and 1871, or in Russia 1905. The Soviets are an institution which does not exist in any ordinary bourgeois parliamentary state and cannot exist side by side with a bourgeois government". (italics by Lenin)

It is clear that the American Zones are a new "type of government, created by the revolution", one which "cannot exist side by side with a bourgeois government". No wonder the capitalists are so determined to crush these Zones! Lenin goes on to explain that which we can expect from these Zones: "They can neither retreat nor stand still. They can exist only by advancing. This is a type of state not invented by the Russians but advanced by the revolution, because the revolution can win in no other way". He goes on to say that this is a "transition to a republic which will establish a stable power without a police and a standing army".

Without doubt, we must encourage these Zones. The success of the revolution depends on this. It provides the working people with valuable training and experience, in preparation for the Dictatorship Of the Proletariat.

During the summer months of 1917, between the time of the February-March revolution and the October revolution, Lenin prepared for the socialist revolution.

The people of Russia were certainly revolutionary, but confused, and with good reason. There were several political parties which claimed to be Marxist, but were not. Technically these are referred to as social chauvinists, socialists in words, chauvinists in deeds. Also referred to as opportunists, or completely lacking in principle. As well, there is no shortage of people who are of the opinion that the theories of Marx and Lenin must be revised. Such people are referred to as revisionists. A few of them are open in their revisionist sentiments, while a great many are not. Those who are subtle in their distortions of the theories of Marx and Lenin, tend to be more dangerous.

As previously mentioned, I am explaining these technical terms for the benefit of the working people, those who have just recently become politically active. These are terms with which we must all become familiar, as otherwise, our lack of knowledge will be used against us.

A similar state of confusion exists today in America, in that there are political parties which claim to be Marxist, while denying the necessity of the Dictatorship Of the Proletariat. Then again, they may just not mention it, as "working people are not talking about this". To this I can only respond that the reason they are not talking about this, is because they are not aware of it! All too often, those same self proclaimed "Marxists" do not even refer to the existence of classes! It is the duty of conscious people, true Marxists, Communists, to raise the level of awareness of the working class, to make them aware of themselves as a class, with interests which are diametrically opposed to the interests of the capitalist class, the billionaires, the bourgeoisie. That is the reason they must be first overthrown and then crushed under the Dictatorship Of the Proletariat.

Now in America, most working people are literate and own computers, or at least have access to "digital devices", as my grandchildren have corrected me. (Thoughtful of them) As that is the case, explaining all this, to the working class, is seventeen times easier, than it was in Russia, 1917.

Yet somehow, Lenin and the Bolsheviks were able to prepare the workers and peasants for socialism, to carry the revolution through to its logical conclusion, in October of 1917. At that time, the Provisional Government was "holed up" in the Winter Palace of the Czar, hiding from the Russian people, the very people they were supposed to be leading. Their leader was a man named Karensky, so it became known as the Karensky regime.

The capitalists were supremely well aware of the revolutionary movement of the people, and further knew that they could not stop it. They also knew that the revolution had its headquarters in Saint Petersburg. (I should mention that it was also referred to as Petrograd) Even though they could not stop the revolution, they knew just the people who could. Those people were the

Germans. That being the case, the Provisional Government determined to surrender the capitol city of Saint Petersburg, to the enemy, the German army!

Working people, take note! In 1917, the Russian capitalists were prepared to commit the most vile act of treason, as a means of staying in power! The Russian soldiers were fighting and dying, at the front, in order to defend their motherland, as they saw it. Those who refused were shot by firing squad. Yet the same people who demanded such great sacrifices, were supreme traitors! This is typical of the capitalists! They do not hesitate to stoop to the lowest depths! They are completely devoid of morality, as well as principle!

Lenin was well aware that the Kerensky government was preparing to surrender Saint Petersburg, and knew that it would make the revolution far more difficult. As that was the case, it was necessary to strike, and strike immediately. This gave rise to the second revolution of 1917, the socialist revolution of October 25, old style calendar, or November 7, new style calendar.

PART 3

INSURRECTION AND THE IMMEDIATE AFTERMATH

In the fall of 1917, it was clear that the Provisional Government of Karensky had to be overthrown, and the working class had to seize power. Yet it is one thing to seize power, and something else entirely to keep that power. If there is one thing the capitalists hate more than each other, it is Communists. As that is the case, Lenin fully expected the capitalists of neighbouring countries, immediately after the revolution, to invade the newly created socialist republic. That begged the question: could a socialist revolution in Russia possibly succeed?

With that question in mind, Lenin read everything that Marx had written, on the subject of the anticipated first successful socialist revolution. In fact, Marx expected that such a revolution could only be successful if it was carried out in several neighbouring countries, at the same time. The German revolution of 1848 had spread to other countries, so that a similar socialist revolution was quite possible. Yet, Marx also considered the possibility of a successful socialist revolution taking place in one country, if the country was big enough.

Lenin had his answer, as Russia is huge and at that time, had a considerable amount of industry. As that was the case, he prepared for an insurrection.

Without doubt, very soon Americans will also be faced with the problem of mounting a proper insurrection. As that is the case, perhaps it is best to quote a few words from the master of the art, Lenin: "To be successful, insurrection must rely not upon conspiracy, and not upon a party, but upon the advanced class. That is the first point. Insurrection must rely upon a *revolutionary upsurge of the people.* That is the second point. Insurrection must rely upon that *turning point* in the history of the growing revolution when the activity of the advanced ranks of the people is at its height, and when the *vacillations* in the ranks of the enemy and *in the ranks of the weak, half hearted and irresolute friends of the revolution* are strongest. That is the third point . . . .Once these conditions exist, however, to refuse to treat insurrection as an *art* is a betrayal of Marxism and a betrayal of the revolution."(italics by Lenin)

Lenin went on to stress the importance that Marx placed on insurrection. It was not something to be entered into lightly, but once entered into, ensure that you have over whelming force at key positions. Also, it is essential to act with the utmost determination. "The defensive is the death of every armed uprising . . . Surprise your antagonists while their forces are scattered, prepare the way for new successes, however small, but prepare daily; keep up the moral superiority which the first successful rising has given to you; rally in this way those vacillating elements to your side which always follow the strongest impulse and which always look out for the safe side; force your enemies to retreat before they can collect their strength against you; in the words of Danton, the greatest master of revolutionary tactics yet known, be audacious, be more audacious, and yet more audacious." (according to Marx)

As yet, we have not arrived at that point, as so many Americans still have faith in the two party system. Countless people are still loyal to Trump, and continue to believe that the election was stolen, even though the government refers to this as "The Big Lie". Those same workers are not prepared to lay down their lives for socialism. Further preparation must be made for the revolution, before an insurrection can be mounted.

This is to say that a great effort is required, on the part of conscious people, those who are aware of the revolutionary theories of Marx and Lenin, to raise the level of awareness of the working class. Literature must be made available to them, in a somewhat popular form, and sent, if only by email. Those who are more familiar with the internet, than I am, know just how this is done.

No doubt most of this revolutionary work will have to be done by women, as they, and minorities, are leading the revolution. Their influence can be felt throughout society, and not just within the working class.

Now two of the most powerful offices in Washington, that of the Vice President, as well as the Speaker of the House, are both occupied by women. As I write this, the Republican Party is conducting a purge, within the House of Representatives. Representative Liz Cheney is being removed from her position of authority within the House, as she recognizes that Biden is the new president. She is being replaced by another woman, that of Elise Stefanik.

As well, within the House of Representatives, there is a faction, referred to as "The Squad". They were initially composed of four women, all minorities. They have since been joined by two others, one woman and one man, also minorities. They are distinguished by their support for the working class. In fact, they are the proletarian headquarters, within the capitol of Washington. As yet, they may not be aware of this. I mention this to drive home the point that the participation of women and minorities, as an indication of the breadth and depth, of the strength, of those people in the revolutionary movement.

In Russia, by the fall of 1917, the level of awareness of the working people had risen to the point that insurrection was called for. Remarkably enough, all of the peasants, which is to say, the poor, middle and rich peasants, were united behind the working class, the proletariat, in opposition to the landlords, the monarchists and the capitalists, the bourgeoisie.

The reason I use the word remarkable, is because the poor peasants, and the vast majority of peasants were dirt poor, are the natural and desirable allies of the workers, the proletariat. The same cannot be said of the middle peasants, as they tend to vacillate. The rich peasants tend not to vacillate, as they are generally the enemies of the proletariat. Yet they joined the revolution, as they too shared a deep hatred of the landlords. In fact, all peasants hated the landlords, with good reason. The landlords gouged all peasants, without exception, and with great enthusiasm. The landlords were also tied to the nobility, generally through blood relations, so that they were staunch supporters of the monarchy. As far as the rich peasants were concerned, it was a revolution against the landlords.

The rich peasants were referred to as kulaks, which means "tight fist" in Russian. They were essentially misers, those who treasure their gold. And gold they did treasure, as they did not trust paper currency. In fact they hoarded their gold, as well as their grain. Gold does not rust, and is practically indestructible. The same cannot be said of grain. If left too long, or if it gets wet, it tends to rot. This did not stop the tight fists from hoarding their grain, in the hopes that starvation would drive up the price of grain, so that they could sell at a very high price. This frequently resulted in the rotting of the grain, while the poor peasants and workers starved.

Yet those same rich peasants, tight fists, joined the workers and poor peasants, in the revolution, as they were determined to overthrow the landlords. As soon as the insurrection overthrew the Provisional Government, the newly created socialist government granted "land to the tiller", which was precisely the thing all peasants wanted, and the alliance was at an end. The tight fists promptly returned to being the bitter enemies of the poor peasants and the proletariat.

I mention this as one more example of warring classes which come together, in times of revolution, because they have a common goal. After that goal is reached, they frequently return to being enemies. The tight fists were no exception. That became clear only after the insurrection. But first, the insurrection had to be carefully planned.

Once Lenin determined that the insurrection had to be carried out immediately, before Karensky could surrender Saint Petersburg, he wasted no time in making preparations. I should point out that at that time, within the Russian military, most of the enlisted personnel were peasants, while most of the officers were the sons of landlords. The soldiers and sailors had no love, and less respect, for their officers. They were strong supporters of the Bolsheviks.

With that in mind, in October of 1917, Lenin called for "a simultaneous offensive on Saint Petersburg, as sudden and as rapid as possible, which must without fail be carried out from within and from without . . . an offensive of the *entire* navy, the concentration of a *gigantic superiority* of forces . . . Our *three* main forces—the fleet, the workers, and the army units—must be so combined as to occupy without fail and to hold *at any cost* a) the telephone exchange; b) the telegraph office; c) the railroad stations d) and above all else, the bridges.

"The *most determined* elements . . . must be formed into small detachments to occupy all the most important points and to *take part* everywhere in all important operations, for example:

> "to encircle and cut off Saint Petersburg; to seize it by a combined attack of the sailors, the workers, and the troops—a task which requires *art and triple audacity;* "to form detachments from the best workers, armed with rifles and bombs, for the purpose of attacking the enemy's 'centres' . . . Their watchword must be: *'Better to die to a man than let the enemy pass!'*

> "Let us hope that if action is decided upon, the leaders will successfully apply the great percepts of Danton and Marx.

> "The success of both the Russian and the world revolution depends on two or three days fighting" (italics by Lenin)

The common people of Russia, the workers and peasants, followed the advice of Lenin, and on November 7, new style calendar, mounted the insurrection. As the leaders of the Provisional Government were cowering in the winter palace of the Czar, the revolutionaries stormed the palace and arrested the government officials. The insurrection was almost bloodless.

As applies to the upcoming American insurrection, it is important to note that Lenin specifically targeted all communication and transportation centres, especially the bridges. These must be occupied and held *at all costs!*

Due to advances in technology, the communications sector will be more difficult to secure, but it can and must be done. In addition to the telephone and telegraph offices, the internet must be shut down. The cell phones must be disabled. The reason for this is quite simple. Given the opportunity, the capitalists will organize a counter attack, with over powering forces. They must not be given that opportunity! Everything depends on "two or three days fighting".

With that in mind, no doubt the government officials who are taken prisoner will resort to any tricks, in order to access communications with the "outside". That includes faking a heart attack, or any other medical condition. The people guarding such prisoners must be resolute. Even if the medical condition is legitimate, better to allow one capitalist to die, rather than risk the failure of the insurrection.

There have also been advances in the transportation sector. We now have some very impressive highways, which makes the occupation of bridges ever more vital. Air travel has also made great strides, so that closing down the airports is necessary. Blocking the runways should not be difficult, as there is no shortage of heavy equipment in those areas. The airborne troops are a consideration, complete with helicopters and paratroopers. Possibly our finest troops should be sent to occupy the military bases.

Within the vipers nest of Washington, it may be best to regard the various government buildings as the American equivalent of the Russian winter palace. That includes the White House, Capitol Hill, the residence of the Senate and House of Representatives, the Supreme Court, and most especially, the Pentagon. Perhaps it would be best to send our finest, shock troops to capture and hold those headquarters of the capitalists. This is not a task for the faint of heart. Bear in mind the words of Lenin. The success of the revolution requires *"triple audacity!"*

For the benefit of those who may tend to waver, may I suggest you bear in mind the alternative. That is one of hunger, cold, unemployment, homelessness, lawlessness, mass murders and countess other joys which are characteristic of capitalism. Before, you had no choice. Now that the revolution is happening, you do have a choice. Be resolute. Choose wisely.

Immediately following the Russian uprising of November 7, 1917, the new government of workers and poor peasants kept their word. The slogan Land to the Tiller, became the law, to the delight of all peasants. The workers gained control over the factories, and the distribution network, such as the railroads. The banks were nationalized, transformed into a single state enterprise. As well, they proposed a just and democratic peace to all the warring nations.

The capitalists, the bourgeoisie, immediately learned the meaning of the term, Dictatorship Of the Proletariat.

PART 4

THE TREATY OF BREST LITOVSK

At the time of the "Second Russian Revolution of 1917", otherwise known as the October Revolution, even though it took place on November 7, new style calendar, the newly formed government of workers and poor peasants faced the disaster, which had been bequeathed to them by capitalism. This included wide spread hunger, homelessness, unemployment, lawlessness, a crumbling infra structure and factories which were idle or barely producing. (sound familiar?) As well, the country was at war with Germany and the Central Powers. It did not help that the Russian army was disintegrating. Even the Russian generals, those who were absolutely not in favour of the revolution, admitted that the Russian army was no longer an effective fighting force. The common soldiers stated it in more practical terms. As they put it, they were "drowning in blood".

Lenin and the Central Committee of the Bolshevik Party, faced the fact that the question of peace was the "burning question" of the day. Accordingly, they took the bull by the horns and called upon all the warring countries to "start immediate negotiations for a just, democratic peace". By that, they made it clear that they wanted peace without annexations or indemnities. An immediate armistice was proposed. This proposal was met with great resistance, even within the Social Democratic Party, as the Communist Party of the time was called, as well as other political parties within the country, and from high ranking members of the Russian military. In particular, the Social Democratic Party had split, so that the breakaway section, the Mensheviks, were merely social chauvinist, opportunists one and all. The true Marxists were referred to as Bolsheviks. Then there were the Socialist Revolutionaries, who had the support of a great many peasants, and for that reason, had to be respected. On the other hand, the Cadets, or Constitutional Democrats, openly opposed the revolution. They were firmly in the camp of the landlords, the nobility, and the capitalists. Even though these various parties hated each other, they were united in their opposition to the workers and poor peasants, led by the Bolsheviks.

Of course, Lenin was well aware of this opposition to the proposal for peace negotiations. Accordingly, on November 22, he issued an order to the troops at the front, one that shocked the Russian generals, to the very core of their being. Such an order, to any modern army, had never before been issued! Here is the text:

> "Soldiers, the cause of peace is in your hands! Do not allow the counter revolutionary generals to frustrate the great cause of peace, place them under guard in order to avert acts of summary justice unworthy of a revolutionary army and to prevent these generals from escaping the trial that awaits them. Maintain the strictest revolutionary and military order.

> "Let the regiments at the front immediately elect representatives to start formal negotiations for an armistice with the enemy.

"The Council of People's Commissars authorizes you to do this.

"Do everything possible to keep us informed of every step in the negotiations. The Council of People's Commissars is alone authorized to sign the final armistice agreement.

"Soldiers, the cause of peace is in your hands! Maintain vigilance, restraint and energy, and the cause of peace will triumph!"

To think that enlisted men were ordered to arrest their own generals, if those generals were thought to be counter revolutionary! Those same soldiers were then authorized to begin peace negotiations! Such actions cannot even be imagined in an army of a capitalist country! In this manner, the soldiers, which is to say the workers and peasants, came to believe that the new socialist government, led by Bolsheviks, Communists, truly cared about them. It was quite a shock. They did not think it was possible.

The only people more surprised than the soldiers, were the officers. They were accustomed to ordering the firing squad, not facing the firing squad! Yet in this manner, the officers also learned.

The Russian soldiers immediately took action, as those were precisely the orders they were anxious to obey. They sent envoys "across the line" and concluded cease fire agreements, so called "soldiers peace treaties", which generally remained in effect until the conclusion of a general armistice.

Still, the opposition to the peace negotiations was intense, even extending to the counter revolutionary Russian generals. The diplomats from the Allied countries of Britain, France and America were dead set against such talks. They refused to even consider the possibility. After considerable diplomatic maneuvering, on December 15, a 28 day cease fire was agreed upon, between Russia and the Central Powers. The only reason that Russia was forced to negotiate a separate peace with the Central Powers, was because the other Allied powers refused to take part. As a result of this, on December 22, the peace conference opened at the town of Brest-Litovsk.

The peace terms put forward by the Central Powers was harsh, as they demanded a great deal of territory, which included Poland, Lithuania, parts of Estonia and Latvia, and a great deal of Ukraine and Byelorussia. The negotiations dragged on for several weeks, with Trotsky as the lead negotiator for the Soviets. His orders were to argue for the best deal that he could, but in case of an ultimatum, to accept it. But Trotsky had his own ideas. His response became known as the "bayonets in the ground" proposal. As he phrased it, "No peace, no war, army demobilized". He then issued a statement that Soviet Russia would not sign a peace treaty, would discontinue the war, and would demobilize the army. This led to a break down of the talks. On February 18, the Germans responded with a massive offensive.

In Saint Petersburg, Lenin immediately attempted some damage control, so that on February 19, a wireless message was sent to the German Government, stating that the Soviet Government was prepared to sign the peace proposal, on the terms the Germans had listed at Brest-Litovsk. The Germans would have none of it.

The German response of February 23 contained even more onerous terms. They demanded huge land concessions, amounting to a third of the Soviet population, as well as half the industry, ninety percent of the coal mines, and several billion rubles in gold. Yet the Soviets accepted, as it was the opinion of

Lenin that to do otherwise would result in the total destruction of Soviet Russia.

Despite the harsh terms of the Treaty, it gave the newly created Soviet republic a breathing space, time to demobilize the old Russian army and create a new, revolutionary Red army. As well, it was then possible to start socialist construction and prepare for the coming battles against internal counter revolution and foreign intervention.

The Treaty of Brest-Litovsk was signed on March 3, 1918.

PART 5

THE CONSTITUENT ASSEMBLY

Now in the interests of clarity, perhaps it would be best to return to the insurrection of November 7, new style calendar, and recap. The existence of so many classes gave rise to different political parties, which represented those classes. The Cadets were strong supporters of the nobility, landlords and the capitalists, and were dead set against the revolution. They were determined to overthrow the new government, and were openly hostile.

Within the government, the Socialist Revolutionaries had the support of a great many peasants, and were of the opinion that it was the peasants who would lead the revolution. That Party was split between the Lefts, who tended to support the Bolsheviks, and the Rights, who tended to be openly hostile. The Social Democratic party, or modern day Communist Party, was split, between the Bolsheviks, led by Lenin, and the Mensheviks. The Mensheviks were social chauvinists. All of these Parties, and factions, had a voice in the new government that was being created, in the aftermath of the revolution.

As the leader of the new government, Lenin had his hands full. The old state apparatus, which had been used by the nobility and capitalists to crush the workers and peasants, had to be destroyed. A new state apparatus had to be created, in order to crush the "desperate and determined" resistance of the capitalists. This new state apparatus is referred to as the Dictatorship Of the Proletariat.

This meant that the Russian army had to be dissolved, and a new, revolutionary, Red Army had to be created. The old Russian army was disintegrating at the time of the revolution, as countless soldiers were merely walking away. They simply could not fight any more.

As long as the cease fire was in effect, this was not a major problem. It became a major problem at the time of the treachery of Trotsky, in that he broke off negotiations, in direct violation of his orders to accept any ultimatum. The Germans then let him know what they thought of his nonsense of "no war, no peace", that everyone should just "stick the bayonets in the ground". The Germans mounted a major offensive, and the Russians had nothing with which to oppose them.

Yet the new government had to be created, and it had to be an alliance of the workers and poor peasants, the common people. After the first revolution of 1917, a bourgeois republic had been created, with the capitalists in charge. Under such a democracy, the Constituent Assembly represents the highest form of democracy. Of course the imperialist republic, headed by Kerensky, had planned to "fix" the election. (now it is even easier to do so)

At that time, under the Kerensky regime, the Bolsheviks had been correct in calling for elections to a Constituent Assembly. At the same time, they had made it clear that a Republic of

Soviets, under the Dictatorship Of the Proletariat, is a higher form of democracy than a bourgeois republic, with a Constituent Assembly.

After the second revolution of 1917, a Soviet Republic had been established, yet the working people had been promised a Constituent Assembly. The problem was that all of the candidates for that political body had been chosen by the Kerensky regime, mainly by the Socialist Revolutionaries, and therefore did not represent the will of the people. This is characteristic of all political bodies, elected under capitalism.

With that in mind, the Bolsheviks did the principled thing and held elections for the Constituent Assembly, after the November 7 Revolution. Of course the Socialist Revolutionaries won the majority of seats in the election, if for no other reason that they had arranged this before hand.

Even under those conditions, the elections were delayed, due to the resistance of the counter revolutionaries. They then accused the Bolsheviks of delaying the election! This is characteristic of reactionaries everywhere. Lies and slander are part of their stock in trade. Working people learned that the only time the capitalists were lying, was when their lips were moving.

From the moment of the creation of the Constituent Assembly, it became clear that it did not represent the will of the people. On the contrary, as it had been created largely by the Socialist Revolutionaries, it was completely counter revolutionary. Even though, as the name implies, they called themselves socialist and revolutionary, they were in the service of the capitalists. They opposed giving land to the peasants, opposed to the nationalization of the banks, opposed to the cancellation of the national debt. Socialist and revolutionary in words only!

As that was the case, the Bolsheviks withdrew from the Constituent Assembly in January of 1918, as a matter of principle. Under those conditions, it was simply not possible to work within such a reactionary organization.

It had been created in the months between the two revolutions of 1917, the February-March revolution, and the November 7 revolution. The working people had no experience of Soviet power, so of course could not choose between capitalism and socialism. Most of them merely chose to vote for the Socialist Revolutionaries, as the least of various evils. No doubt a great many Americans can understand that, all too well!

It was only after the November 7 revolution, which gave birth to a socialist republic, in the form of the Dictatorship Of the Proletariat, that all working people were able to learn, from their own experience, that the Bolsheviks meant what they said. To the utter astonishment of all, the peasants were indeed given title to the land they were tilling! The banks were nationalized! The national debt was cancelled! A cease fire was declared and peace negotiations were under way! Working people were being supplied with bread! The promise of the Bolsheviks for "Peace, Land and Bread", was being fulfilled! Yet the Constituent Assembly was opposed to all this!

It soon became apparent to the working people, that the Constituent Assembly had served its purpose. Under socialism, there is no place for such an establishment. The previous ruling classes, which in that case was the landlords, the nobility and the capitalists, had been overthrown but still existed. They were still a force with which to be reckoned! They were determined to restore their "paradise lost", at the expense of the working people, of course, so that a force had to be created, in order to crush their "desperate and determined" resistance. That force, that state apparatus, was in the alliance of the workers and poor peasants, the Dictatorship Of the Proletariat.

The Constituent Assembly was dead set opposed to this! It was a completely reactionary organization, and had to be destroyed. It was dissolved in January of 1918, not because the Bolsheviks did not have a majority of members, but because it was counter revolutionary.

PART 6

THE DICTATORSHIP OF
THE PROLETARIAT

Not everyone was wildly enthusiastic with the new socialist republic, or at least not in the form of the Dictatorship Of the Proletariat. Voices were raised that it was too "undemocratic", so that as early as November 11, a mere few days after the insurrection, there were calls for a "uniform socialist government".

These complaints had to be taken very seriously, as they originated from an organization referred to as Vikzhel, the All Russian Central Committee of the Railwaymen's Trade Union, which was dominated by the Mensheviks and Socialist Revolutionaries. As that was the case, it was solidly counter revolutionary. Yet the smooth functioning of the trains was essential to the success of the revolution. Only the trains could ensure the transfer of manufactured goods from the factories in the cities, to the countryside, to be exchanged for grain and wood. Without the grain, the people would starve, and without the wood, the factories would sit idle.

This call for a "uniform socialist government", or some such nonsense, is precisely what we can expect, immediately after the American Revolution, after we establish the Dictatorship Of the Proletariat. The same people who are now opposed to socialism, will face the fact that it exists, and "change their tune". As yet, we have no idea of the expression they will create, although it could be "pure democracy" or "pure socialism" or even "pure social democracy". For that reason, we had best be prepared. With that in mind, we can examine a similar situation.

In the summer of 1917, Lenin was consumed with preparations for the approaching socialist revolution. In order to prepare the common people, the workers and poor peasants, for the Dictatorship Of the Proletariat, he wrote State and Revolution. It is every bit as relevant today, as at the time it was first written. All American workers should read it.

Lenin makes the point that the state, or the government apparatus, came into existence at the same time classes came into existence. He quotes Engels as saying, "these classes with conflicting economic interests" gave birth to a "power seemingly standing above society . . . arisen out of society but placing itself above it, and increasingly alienating itself more and more from it, is the state".

Lenin goes on to say "The state arises when, where, and to the extent that class antagonisms objectively *cannot* be reconciled. And conversely, the existence of the state proves that the class antagonisms are irreconcilable." The antagonisms between the working class, the proletariat, and the capitalist class, the bourgeoisie, are irreconcilable.

Just as the first classes to appear were slaves and slave owners, complete with different class interests, so too the classes of today have different class interests. The slave owners of yesteryear worked their slaves as hard as possible, while the capitalists of today work their wage slaves, proletarians, as hard as possible. It is in their best interests to do so! It was also in the best interests of the slaves to rebel, just as it is in the best interests of the wage slaves to rebel. And just as the slave owners set up a state apparatus to keep their slaves subjugated, so too the modern day capitalists have set up a state apparatus to keep their wage slaves subjugated.

Every Marxist, or Communist, is supremely well aware of this. By contrast, there are the social chauvinists, socialists in words, chauvinists in deeds, who attempt to "correct" Marx, in such a way as to make it appear that the state is an organ for the *reconciliation* of classes. Even though Marx maintains the the state could not arise or maintain itself, if it was possible to reconcile classes. He made it quite clear that the state is an organ of *class rule*, an organ for the *oppression* of one class by another. In this manner it creates something commonly referred to as "law and order".

Immediately after the American revolution, we will almost certainly have to create a coalition government, composed of Communists and non Communists, especially those who refer to themselves as Social Democrats. These people are our friends, and must be treated as such. It is very likely that many of them will be of the opinion that Marx was mistaken, especially if they fall under the influence of the social chauvinists. They may call for a government that represents all classes, a "universal democracy". The error of their ways must be explained to them.

The state is nothing more than an apparatus set up by one class, in order to suppress another class. Under capitalism, we have the democratic republic, which represents the dictatorship of the bourgeoisie. They, the capitalists, the bourgeoisie, rule. That is just a fact. Another fact is that the one and only way to emancipate labour from the yoke of capital is to replace this dictatorship with the *Dictatorship Of the Proletariat!*

As Lenin quite clearly pointed out, "It is only the Dictatorship Of the Proletariat that can emancipate humanity from the oppression of capital, from the lies, falsehood and hypocrisy of bourgeois democracy—democracy *for the rich*—and establish democracy *for the poor,* that is, make the blessings of democracy *really* accessible to the workers and poor peasants, whereas now, (even in the most democratic—*bourgeois*—republic) the blessings of democracy are, *in fact,* inaccessible to the vast majority of working people". (italics by Lenin)

No doubt all working people can relate to that! The "law" does not apply to the rich! They can commit the most terrible acts of violence, even against women and children, and get away with this! The technical term for this is "bourgeois democracy".

Even after the revolution, classes will continue to exist. The capitalists, the billionaires, the bourgeoisie, will be anxious to regain their "paradise lost". They will stoop to any depth, any deception, resort to any lie, any slander, in order to regain their wealth and power. They are completely devoid of principle and morality. They must be crushed.

Engels made this quite clear, in a letter he wrote to Bebel, concerning some such similar nonsense, that of a "free people's state". As he phrased it, "As therefore, the state is only a transitional institution which is used in the struggle, in the revolution, in order to hold down one's adversaries by force, it is pure nonsense to talk of a free people's state; so long as the proletariat still *uses* the state, it does not use it in the interest of freedom, buy to hold down its adversaries" (italics by Engels)

The first impression of a "uniform socialist government" or of a "pure social democracy", may sound harmless. It most definitely is not. It will lead to the domination of the ideology of the capitalists, the bourgeois, and to the restoration of capitalism. Lenin explains the reason for this is quite simple, "that bourgeois ideology is far older in origin than Social Democratic ideology; that it is more fully developed and because it possesses *immeasurably* more opportunities for being distributed." (italics by Lenin, as at that time Communists were referred to as Social Democrats)

Immediately after the revolution, the old state apparatus, which was set up by the capitalists, as a means of crushing the working class, must be destroyed. A new state apparatus must be created, in order to crush the capitalists, the billionaires, the bourgeoisie. This new state apparatus is referred to as the Dictatorship Of the Proletariat. That is the one and only way to ensure that the capitalists do not return to power.

All talk of "pure democracy" or "universal democracy" is that which we refer to as an oxymoron, a contradiction in terms. These include such expressions as "military intelligence", as the military is anything but intelligent, "secret bombing", as it is not possible to bomb people and keep it a secret, "holy war", as war is anything but holy. So too, democracy is a method of rule, in which one class crushes another class. There is nothing "pure" or "universal" about that! The capitalists, the bourgeois, must be destroyed, absolutely crushed, or they will return to power. The one and only way to do this is through the Dictatorship Of the Proletariat.

PART 7

THE RUSSIAN CIVIL WAR

Immediately after the insurrection of November 7, the counter revolutionaries wasted no time in attempting to overthrow the new government. The Bolsheviks invited other political parties to take part in the new socialist government, and the Left Socialist Revolutionaries agreed, as they were closely allied with the Bolsheviks. The Right Socialist Revolutionaries and the Mensheviks proposed to begin negotiations with the Provisional Government of Karensky, but this was rejected. At that point, the Right Socialist Revolutionaries and the Mensheviks walked out, choosing to not take part in any socialist government.

In the interest of forming a socialist government, the Bolsheviks recognized that the Socialist Revolutionaries had the support of a great many peasants. With that in mind, Lenin carefully read the agrarian platform of the Socialist Revolutionaries. He did not entirely agree with it, but as this was the program the peasants wanted, so be it. He had no doubt that in time, the peasants would solve the agrarian problem in their own way. It was in their best interests to do so! They did not need someone sitting in Saint Petersburg telling them how to farm!

For that reason, they adopted the agrarian platform of the Socialist Revolutionaries, in its entirety. Those same Socialist Revolutionaries then accused the Bolsheviks of stealing their platform! Sore winners! They got exactly what they wanted, and then complained bitterly!

The counter revolutionary officers of the Russian military were dealt with promptly, as the troops under their command were ordered to arrest any officer who was suspected of being counter revolutionary, and that included the generals. Such officers then faced a revolutionary court, and if found guilty, were sentenced to face the firing squad.

Karensky was the leader of the former Provisional Government, and one of the members who escaped arrest on November 7. He promptly attempted to lead troops against the new Soviet Republic, but had no success in Saint Petersburg. He did manage some limited success in Moscow, but was soon forced out.

The counter revolutionaries within the country were aided by the international imperialists. Their goal was to restore the power of the landlords and capitalists, in order to squeeze from the workers and peasants the interest on the loans the Czar had made. At the same time, they were hoping to extinguish the revolutionary fire that was raging all across Russia, and threatening to engulf the world.

It may come as a surprise to most working people to realize that the capitalists are well aware that revolutionary motion tends to spread, and not just across a single country, but around the world. The experience of the recent Occupy Movement provides us with a very clear cut example of that. We can expect the current American revolution to also spread to other countries.

Bear in mind that the Occupy Movement failed to achieve most of its goals, if only because it lacked the proper leaders. No doubt the astute reader may suspect that this is a none too subtle hint that the leaders, to whom I am referring, were not Communists. True enough. Instead, they were well meaning people, honest, determined, self sacrificing individuals, those who took a stand on principle and were prepared to go to jail for their beliefs. Just as well, as that is precisely where they were sent.

The working class is grateful for the service of all the veterans of the Occupy Movement. No doubt they have been tempered in the conflict, and no longer have any illusions. By now they are well aware that our democratically elected leaders serve the capitalists, and only the capitalists. The politicians in Washington do not represent the people who elected them. They serve the class of people whom are referred to as the bourgeoisie, the monopoly capitalists, the billionaires.

It is also very likely that most of the leaders of the Occupy Movement, as well as many of the people who took part in that protest movement, were members of the middle class. As such, they were almost certainly well educated, class conscious, aware of the revolutionary theories of Marx and Lenin. Yet there is a big difference between being aware of certain theories and acting upon them. Perhaps they thought those theories were something of a curiosity, rather quaint. Perhaps they thought that the system could indeed be "changed from within". Perhaps they thought that they could enact significant reforms, even under capitalism. Perhaps now they are kicking themselves for being so naive.

To such people, most of whom are females, I am sure, I can only respond that there is no need to be too hard on yourselves. Others will do that for you! All Americans are bombarded with bourgeois propaganda all their lives, day and night. The message, in various forms, all boils down to the same thing: "America is the greatest country in the world". After hearing that message so many times, people begin to believe it! Advertising works! That is the reason so many companies spend so much money on hawking their product! That is also the reason so many politicians spend mountains of money on campaign ads! What is more, for that very reason, it is so difficult to start a revolution in a highly industrialized country, a cultured country!

Yet now the situation has changed dramatically, as I am sure all veterans of the Occupy Movement are well aware. The twin crises of the virus and the depression have devastated the middle class. A great many have been ruined, frequently cast aside by the same corporations to which those people have devoted their lives. Now bitter and disillusioned, they have been forced to join the ranks of the working class. Yet they bring with them their awareness of classes, as well as their awareness of the revolutionary theories of Marx and Lenin. Welcome, comrades, fellow intellectuals! Now is the time to cast aside your bitterness and frustration, to focus your anger and hatred on destroying the class of people who have crushed and exploited all others! Of course that class is the bourgeoisie, and you can perform a most valuable service in ensuring their destruction.

The working class people, the proletariat, are doing their best, rising up and forming Autonomous Zones, even if not in the geographical sense. They have learned that to occupy an area merely results in a response, by the government, of overpowering force. (sound familiar?) So now they are carrying out reforms, in opposition to the government, without setting up a zone. As they are unaware of the revolutionary theories of Marx and Lenin, they can go no further. That is where you come in.

Only intellectuals can create a truly American Communist Party. By that I mean a Party which advocates the Dictatorship Of the Proletariat. That is the "touchstone" of a true Marxist, as all other parties which claim to be Marxist, or Communist, but deny the necessity of such a Dictatorship, are merely revisionists, social chauvinists, socialists in words, chauvinists in deeds. They are among the most devoted servants of the capitalists.

These people are not to be confused with those who are fighting for reforms of one sort or another, political or economic. They may consider themselves to be democrats or socialists, or democratic socialists. They must be treated with the utmost respect and consideration, as they are the natural and desirable friends of the working class. A few of their leaders may be less than friendly, but it is best to distinguish between the rank and file and the leaders. If possible, avoid confrontation with the leaders, as that would only serve to alienate the rank and file.

As the women are leading the revolution, perhaps you ladies can take some inspiration in the thought of holding certain men accountable. Of course I am referring to those who have assaulted and degraded women in the past. By and large, they are "immune from prosecution", to use the legal term, as in most cases, the statute of limitations protects these lowlifes. In all cases, they are able to hide behind a battery of high priced lawyers. The same is true of those who have molested children. This is not too surprising as the same bourgeois who write the laws, are the same bourgeois who rape women and molest children! But then I am sure you are well aware of this!

That is characteristic of all capitalist countries. That is not characteristic of all countries which practice scientific socialism. Of course that is a reference to the Dictatorship Of the Proletariat. The Dictatorship is just that, a Dictatorship, over the bourgeois, by the Proletariat. The bourgeois will soon have no rights. They will be crushed. They will not be able to hide behind an army of lawyers. No laws will protect them. The statute of limitations is about to go the way of the dodo bird. Very soon, they can, and they will, face "their accusers", which is to say you ladies, or the mothers of the children they have molested. At that point, the accusers will decide their fate. Should you choose to forgive them, all well and good. Then again, should you choose to hold them accountable, then you ladies can determine their punishment. One good turn deserves another!

To return to Russia, immediately after the November 7 revolution. The internal enemies were the supporters of the landlords, the monarchy and the capitalists. As well, the rich peasants, the kulaks or tight fists, were determined to hoard their grain, in the hopes that the starvation of the workers and poor peasants would drive up the price of grain, so that they could "make a killing". Then there were the social chauvinists, and in particular the Right Socialist Revolutionaries and the Mensheviks, who controlled the railway workers union. All were determined to sabotage the revolution.

On the external front, there were the imperialists of Germany, Japan, Britain, France, Italy and America. At first, the Germans were the most immediate threat, as they bordered Soviet Russia. It helped that they were preoccupied with fighting the imperialists of Britain, France and America. This was just as well, as Soviet Russia was practically helpless, with no army to oppose any invasion. That was the reason they accepted the Treaty of Brest-Litovsk.

That Treaty cost the Russian Soviet Republic dearly. It came at a very high price, but Lenin and the Communists were convinced that it gave the country their one chance at survival. It bought them time. Each day was precious, allowing the Communists to build a new socialist republic. The common people, the workers and peasants, had no reason to trust any government officials. As they had been lied to all their lives, who could blame them? Yet the peasants had been told that they owned the land they were tilling, so that the crop they harvested belonged to them. The best part of the crop did not go to the landlords! The workers, the proletarians, found themselves working an eight hour day, and in control of their workplace, whether factory, mill, mine or railroad, for example. To their utter astonishment, they found that the Bolsheviks, the Communists, meant exactly what they said! It took some getting used to, but then the working people began to trust the new socialist government.

At that point, many of the peasants, those whom had deserted the army, returned to the military, but not as the Russian soldiers of old, but as Red Army troops. They were prepared to fight and die for the new Soviet Socialist Republic.

After the new Socialist Republic secured peace with Germany, that still left the imperialists of Britain, France, Japan, Italy and America. Much as each and every one of them, desperately wanted to destroy that Socialist Republic, "geographical considerations" was not in their favour. They were broken hearted that they had no common frontiers with Russia, which meant that invasion was out of the question. So they decided that the next best thing was to incite all the countries neighbouring Soviet Russia, to go to war with Soviet Russia.

With that in mind, in August of 1919, it was reported that the British Secretary of State for War, Winston Churchill, made a speech to the British Parliament. At that time, he bragged that no less than fourteen countries were involved in crushing the new upstart socialist republic. He was referring to the fact that the imperialist countries of Britain, America, France, Japan and Italy were arming and equipping the republics which neighboured Soviet Russia, that of Finland, Estonia, Latvia, Lithuania, Poland, the Ukraine, Georgia, Azerbaijan, Armenia and "Kolchakia and Denikia"

The last two items in quotations was probably a reference to the territory controlled by Kolchak and Deniken.

Clearly, the various imperialists were determined to destroy this upstart socialist republic.

Even after the defeat of Germany on November 11, 1918, the British maintained troops in Europe, for perhaps a year, in the interest of crushing the upstart Soviet Socialist Republic. That did not work out quite the way the British imperialists had planned, as the troops could not understand the reason they were still fighting, when the war was over! Worse, they were becoming "contaminated" with the heretical idea of socialism! Rather than "containing" Bolshevism, as was the name of Communism, they were spreading it! The British soldiers were deeply impressed by the democratic rights that were granted to the common people of Soviet Russia, by the fact that farmers owned their own land, and that the workers controlled the factories where they worked! Worse, they thought such a system would work just fine in Britain! The nerve of some people!

The Russian civil war raged for three years. At one point, most of the country was occupied by the Whites, as the counter revolutionaries referred to themselves, so that the Reds, the Russian Revolutionaries, were fighting a war on five fronts. The invading troops, the Whites, were armed with the finest equipment and weapons, supplied mainly by Britain, France and America, while the defending Red Army troops were fighting with whatever was available.

From a strictly military stand point, it should have been a "cake walk" for the Whites. It was not. The common soldiers of the Whites were something less than enthusiastic in fighting the Reds. Most of them were peasants, while the officers were the sons of landlords. Members of different classes. The class of landlords considers the class of peasants to be completely contemptible. As most of the soldiers were peasants, and the officers were landlords, this contempt spread to the military. The officers disciplined the soldiers with great brutality, and that included flogging.

As a result of this, to phrase it in military terms, the "morale" of the troops was low. It is one thing to provide soldiers with the finest arms and equipment. It is something else entirely to motivate them to fight the enemy! The American imperialists were reminded of this in the war they waged in Viet Nam!

By contrast, the morale of the Red Army was high. They were defending their home land and their new socialist way of life. Even though most of the soldiers were peasants, their ranks were bolstered by a great many workers, proletarians. These workers were accustomed to being self disciplined, and helped to encourage their peasant stock brethren.

The Soviet high command assisted the troops in every manner. A supreme effort was made to maintain the two main cities of Saint Petersburg and Moscow, to keep them from being captured by the Whites. The factories in the cities focused on producing that which the troops needed. A great many women went to work in the factories, which freed up a great many men, for the front. In short, the whole country mobilized, in order to defend the new Socialist Soviet Republic.

As Lenin later stated, a modern "miracle" took place, in that the workers and peasants rose up against the attacks of the land owners and capitalists, financed by the imperialists of foreign countries. The lesson here is that in times of revolution, the common people are capable of overcoming enormous obstacles.

PART 8

THE NEW ECONOMIC POLICY

It was only in 1921 that Lenin and the Soviets could turn their attention to economic development. Up until that time, they had been focused on the war. First the war with Germany and the Central Powers, and then the civil war in Soviet Russia, fighting the "Whites", the counter revolutionary interventionists.

Lenin faced the fact that Russia was a most "backward" country. This is to say that, from an economic viewpoint, it was one hundred years behind the most highly industrialized countries of the world, such as Britain and America. In other words, the state of industrial development, of Russia, was at the level of those two countries, one hundred years previously. As well, the population of Russia had about the same proportion of peasants, about three quarters, as those two countries had, also one hundred years ago. This was completely unacceptable.

Lenin was supremely well aware that the peace treaties which Soviet Russia had managed to conclude, with various countries, was strictly temporary. No capitalist country is about to allow a socialist country to peacefully coexist. It was just a matter of time before the neighbouring capitalist countries gathered their forces, and once again attacked Soviet Russia. They had to be prepared.

This meant that Soviet Russia had to develop industry, to the level enjoyed by Britain and America, and they had to do this within ten years. That which had taken one hundred years, for the capitalist countries to accomplish, the socialist Soviet Russia had to accomplish, but in ten years. That was a tall order. But then, it was either that, or be destroyed.

With that in mind, Lenin realized that drastic changes had to be made. His solution, was referred to as the New Economic Policy, or NEP. The idea was to take advantage of the great abundance of natural resources, with which Russia was blessed, and use that to attract international capital. In particular, the country had vast reserves of timber, oil and coal, among other things. Then the capitalists of other countries were offered "concessions", in that they could harvest those items, and make a huge profit. In return, the Russians would receive badly needed machinery, which they needed in order to develop their industry and harvest the remainder. That was the only way to raise the Russian technology to the modern level, that of the British and Americans, and quickly. At the same time, the government substituted a tax for the requisitioning of grain, so that the peasants could sell their surplus grain on the open market.

Of course there was considerable opposition to this change of economic policy, as so many devoted Communists considered this to be a step back from socialism, a retreat to capitalist. In this, they were absolutely correct. Yet it had to be done. Lenin referred to this as an orderly retreat.

Lest there be any misunderstanding, perhaps it would be best to allow Lenin to explain this in his own words: "The New Economic Policy means substituting a tax for the requisitioning of food; it means reverting to capitalism to a certain extent . . . Concessions to foreign capitalists . . . and leasing enterprises to private capitalists definitely means restoring capitalism, and this is part and policy of the New Economic Policy; for the abolition of the surplus food appropriation system means allowing the peasants to trade freely in their surplus agricultural produce, in whatever is left over after the tax is collected—and the tax takes only a small share of that produce. The peasants constitute a huge section of our population and of our entire economy, and that is why capitalism must grow out of this soil of free trading."

Lenin went on to explain that as capitalism flourishes, industrial production will grow—it was almost at a stand still, so that the proletariat disappeared. On the other hand, "The restoration of capitalism would mean the restoration of a proletarian class engaged in the production of socially useful material values in big factories employing machinery, and not in profiteering . . . which is inevitable when our industry is in a state of ruin."

It is truly remarkable to think that, in a truly socialist country, which is to say one that embraced the Dictatorship Of the Proletariat, the Communist leaders allowed capitalism to flourish. They took a principled stand, knowing full well that it was the one and only way to provide the vast majority of people, the peasants, with an improvement in their standard of living. They were also well aware that the capitalists were guaranteed to take advantage of this, to attempt to restore capitalism.

Lenin and the Communists had faith in the peasants. As he phrased it, "the proletarian state power, with the support of the peasantry, will prove capable of keeping a proper rein on those gentlemen, the capitalists, so as to direct capitalism along state channels and to create a capitalism that will be subordinate to the state and serve the state".

As can be well imagined, the Russian workers were not at all enthusiastic concerning the idea of working, once again, for the capitalists. As they saw it, they did not throw out their own capitalists, just so that they could import some foreign capitalists! These sentiments were not confined to the workers. Even a great many members of the Communist Party were of this opinion.

It required some patient explanation, to the effect that these measures were only temporary. The workers, those who were employed by the foreign capitalists, would be covered by union protection, be well paid, and with considerable benefits. Everyone had to look at the bigger picture. The country had to become highly industrialized, as it was just a matter of time before the capitalists invaded. Either industrialize or be crushed. It was just that simple.

As previously mentioned, most of the people were peasants, and the vast majority of them were illiterate. But then they had no electricity. This had to change, and that alone was a huge project. The granting of concessions to the foreign capitalists went a long way towards building electric generation plants. The isolation of the peasants, and their ignorance, went hand in hand, and this led to their resentment. Providing them with electricity went a long way towards overcoming this resentment.

If nothing else, this helps to illustrate the fact that it is exceptionally difficult to establish scientific socialism, the Dictatorship Of the Proletariat, in a predominantly peasant country. It is absolutely essential for the working class, the proletariat, to unite with the poor peasant. It is much less difficult to build socialism, in a country which is already highly industrialized. Americans, take note!

In the case of Russia, after the revolution, the workers took over the factories, mills, mines and railroads, for example. Then the workers were obligated to produce, and supply manufactured goods, to the whole country, with everything that was needed. In the case of the peasants, those who constitute the majority of the population, it was necessary to transport, by rail or river vessels, the manufactured goods. In return, the peasants would provide the workers with their surplus produce. Under the New Economic Policy, the peasants were allowed to provide the workers with part of their surplus produce, and sell the remainder. This was referred to as "tax in kind", and was meant as a temporary measure.

The fact of the matter is that small scale farming is quite inefficient. After the revolution, the peasants were granted title to the land they were tilling, so that the number of small peasant farms grew dramatically. In fact, there were more small farms after the revolution, than before the revolution. Yet they produced less grain, than before the revolution.

Just as large scale industry is far more efficient than small scale industry, so too large scale farming is far more efficient than small scale farming. Yet the peasants had to learn this from their own experience, and could not be forced into it. The goal of socialism was to create large scale tracts of farming land, which could only be done if the individual peasants pooled their land, forming communes. Then the people who worked on these communes would no longer be peasants, as they no longer owned the land, but worked on the land. Rural proletarians.

As this transition to socialism was taking place, there was one unexpected development, and it was serious. Americans will soon be facing this same problem. In Russia, as the country made the transition to a peace time economy, countless soldiers were demobilized. This resulted in a considerable amount of banditry, as the returning soldiers found themselves out of work and frustrated.

Immediately after the upcoming American revolution, we can expect a similar situation. The American military will be disbanded, and a great many personnel will be returning home, looking for work. We had best be prepared. As military personnel, they must be respected. They made great sacrifices, serving their country. It was the capitalists who took advantage of them. We must not hold their military service against the soldiers. Instead, we must hold the capitalists responsible for any and all war crimes.

As we attempt to rebuild the country, there will be a period of transition, between capitalism and socialism. We can expect a certain amount of confusion. A great deal of planning is required. The specialists, by whom I mean the economists, for example, are accustomed to planning production, but with the interests of profit in mind. They are going to have to change their focus, to the needs of the common people. This will happen, but not overnight. Old habits are difficult to break. Yet with a little persuasion, they will come around to our way of thinking. Or they will wish they had.

The point is that, in order to build socialism, something more is required than production alone. The production must be planned.

PART 9

PLANNED PRODUCTION AND THE TROTSKY OPPOSITION

In January of 1924, Lenin died, as a result of complications brought about as a result of being shot by a member of the Socialist Revolutionaries, in 1918. Of course this gave rise to a power struggle within the top ranks of the Communist Party. Fortunately, as a true Marxist and devoted to Lenin, as well as the Dictatorship Of the Proletariat, it was Stalin who emerged victorious.

I should point out that in 1922, several independent socialist republics came together to form the Union of Soviet Socialist Republics, other wise known as the Soviet Union. As that was their official name, that is the name I will use.

Stalin carried on the New Economic Policy of Lenin, for several years. In this way, the Soviet Union became industrialized, due to the capitol influx from the western powers, mainly American corporations, and the technical assistance they provided. All of these corporations were richly rewarded, paid in Russian gold. The western capitalists should be given credit for the "miracle" of transforming Soviet Russia, from a predominantly peasant country, to a highly industrialized modern country. What is more, they managed this in record time. Mind you, they were richly rewarded, becoming supremely wealthy in the process. Thank you, western capitalists!

Lenin was absolutely correct, in that his New Economic Policy dramatically raised the living standard of the peasants. The peasants in turn trusted their new government leaders, as they were persuaded that for once, they had a government that cared about them. Very few of them, mainly the tight fists, were at all anxious to return to the previous state of capitalism. The vast majority of peasants listened to their new Communist leaders. More to the point, they witnessed the new agricultural communes. The people who worked on those communes were no longer peasants, at the mercy of the weather, bugs, flooding, poor seed and fluctuations in the price of grain. They were working together, sharing their draft animals and tractors, and producing far more. The peasants became convinced, from experience, that communal farming was far better than peasant farming. So a great many of them pooled their land and equipment and became rural workers.

These communes produced a great deal more, with a great deal less workers. As a result of this, a great many former peasants became available for work in the industrial centres which were springing up, all over the country, thanks largely to the foreign capitalists. They were also paying union rates, which tended to be far more than most peasants could ever dream of earning. There was no shortage of people who were prepared to work for the capitalists, foreign or domestic!

By 1928, Stalin and the Communists decided that it was time to move on to the next stage of economic development. This became knows as the "Great Break". The New Economic Policy had served its purpose, and now it was time to move on to planned production. This marked the beginning of the first Five Year Plan.

The significance of this "planned production" cannot be over stated. Under capitalism, we have that which is referred to as the "law of supply and demand". The capitalists swear by this! Working people tend to swear at it, and with good reason.

Under capitalism, at the time in which a commodity is scarce and in demand, the capitalists invest their capital in factories, as the price of the commodity is also high. They then hire workers and run their factories nonstop, pumping out as much product as possible, as quickly as possible. As the price of the product is high, this makes complete sense, and the capitalists make a handsome profit. It also makes sense that the market is soon flooded, the price of the product drops, and the product sells for a loss. This is called "boom to bust". They refer to this as the "cost of doing business", and lay off the workers. The working people have another name for it, which does not bear repeating.

The only thing the capitalists have to lose is their capital, and they tend to have a great surplus of that. By contrast, workers tend to relocate to wherever the jobs are—what choice is there? Then it is a matter of finding a place to live, moving the family, perhaps buying a house, all at high price, because as the demand goes up, so do the prices. Then the capitalist shuts down the factory, as it is losing money. Poor capitalist. But now the workers are unemployed, possibly stuck with a huge mortgage, facing bankruptcy and no place to go.

As I live in a remote area, this becomes sharp and clear. I am told that the price of lumber has now increased to double that of the previous year. So now the capitalists are investing their capital in saw mills, firing them up and running them almost "twenty four-seven". This means running two ten hour shifts, Monday to Thursday, and two twelve hour shifts, Friday to Sunday. It does not take a genius to figure out that the mills are shut down a mere sixteen hours a week, for clean up. Nor does it take a genius to figure that in a short time, the market will be flooded, as the capitalists are very good at pumping out vast quantities of lumber, in a very short time.

At that time, the market will be flooded, the price of lumber will drop, and the capitalists will be laying off the workers. This is typical.

Another example comes to mind. The price of coal was high, so that a small town was built in a very remote location. By remote, I mean that the town had to first be logged out. Then the houses and business centre was built, as well as the railroad. Miners from all across the country were hired, moved to the new town and bought the houses. Then several years later, the price of coal dropped, the mine shut down, and guess what happened? The good old "law of supply and demand".

Stalin and the Communists were determined to break this "law of supply and demand", which is based on the profit motive. Instead, they set reasonable goals, based on planning ahead for five years. The first five year plan was for the years 1928-1932. They decided to focus on developing heavy industry, such as iron and steel, machine tools, electric power and transport. This was all taking place because they knew that it was just a matter of time, before their capitalist neighbours invaded, once again. The idea was that with iron and steel, as well as steel tools, they could produce the armoured vehicles needed to repel the enemy invaders. Then too, people had to eat, so that the creation of communes was accelerated. Both grain and manufactured goods have to be transported, so that the system of railroads and river barges was expanded. As well, both industry and people need electricity, so that a great many hydro electric dams were created.

The Soviets even set themselves the goal of abolishing adult illiteracy! They did not entirely succeed, but a great many peasants learned how to read and write, and a whole new world was opened up to them. Of course, literacy is a great bonus, when working in an industry. More so than when growing crops, as any farmer can testify.

The first Five Year Plan was a great success, in that all the goals were reached in four years. To put this in perspective, the rest of the world was mired in the Great Depression, with countless factories and mines idle, massive unemployment and widespread despair. The world of capitalism was rotting, while the Socialist Soviet Union was booming, making steady progress! Who says history does not repeat itself! We are now mired in a Second Great Depression!

The second Five Year Plan became the 1933-1937 Plan, and it too was wildly successful. By the end of that second Plan, the industrial production of Soviet Russia was the equal of Britain or America! The Soviet Socialist Republic had managed to do that which the capitalists had thought to be impossible. They accomplished, in ten years, that which it had taken the capitalists, one hundred year to manage! The Soviet Union was industrialized!

It should come as no surprise to any one to learn that these years, within the Soviet Union, were not what we would call "smooth sailing". On the contrary, within the Communist Party, there was deep division. In particular, Trotsky was a very busy lad.

Even though socialism was being built and strengthened in one country, the Soviet Union, Trotsky maintained that it could not be done. He was determined to spread revolution to all countries. He insisted that the revolution in the Soviet Union had to be tied to the "development of a world socialist revolution", otherwise known as a "permanent revolution".

At that time, in the Soviet Union, the name of the Party had been changed to the Communist Party, (Bolshevik), and within the Party, there was a Central Committee. It was the Central Committee which appointed a Political Bureau, or Politburo. It was the Politburo which made day to day political decisions, which later had to be ratified by the Central Committee.

Remarkably enough, Trotsky was a member of that Politburo, and a highly skilled trouble maker. It was not until 1926 that the Central Committee decided they had enough, and expelled Trotsky from the Politburo. The following year, 1927, he was further expelled from the Communist Party, along with those who had supported him. He was then exiled to Siberia, and then, in 1929, either allowed to leave the country, or expelled from the country.

It was only several years later, in 1937, the Soviets learned that Trotsky had more followers than they had suspected. There was a plot, within the highest reaches of the Soviet military, to overthrow the Soviet government. Apparently the conspirators were working with the German Nazis, and were promised the full support of the Nazis, in return for the Ukraine. This conspiracy was led by Marshal Tukhachevsky.

No doubt this conspiracy had been simmering for a few years. At the time of the revolution, twenty years earlier, it was necessary to disband the old Russian army, that which had been used to crush the working people, and create a new, revolutionary Red army, in order to defend the newly created Soviet Republic. Yet the new Red army needed officers, and the only people who were qualified to lead, were the men whom had previously been officers in the old Russian army.

Within the old Russian army, almost all the enlisted personnel had been peasants, while almost all the officers had been members of the landlord class, with ties to the nobility. Tukhachevsky was no exception, as he was of noble birth. He was also a highly skilled officer, and as such, rose rapidly through the ranks of the new Red army.

Now that capitalism has long since been restored in the former Soviet Union, it is difficult to get the facts concerning the case. The Russian capitalists are every bit as determined to distort history, as are the American capitalists. The last thing any capitalist wants is for the working people to become aware of their revolutionary history! God forbid that they should get any bright ideas! Yet the fact remains that Tukhachevsky and eight other high ranking generals were arrested. The Soviet Supreme Court convened a special military tribunal to try all nine officers, on the charge of treason. This is referred to as the Trotskyist Anti Soviet Military Organization trial. All defendants confessed, were convicted and shot.

There is a lesson to be learned from this. Even after the forthcoming American revolution, classes will continue to exist. The capitalists, the billionaires, the bourgeoisie, are not about to "ride off into the sunset". That would never occur to them! They are not about to "resign themselves to their fate"! Their fury and hatred will rise to a fever pitch! In order to "regain their paradise lost", they will resort to any lies, any slander, they will stoop to any depths, in order to return to power. Further, as long as they "live and breath", they are not about to stop plotting.

Just as Tukhachevsky and his followers bided their time for twenty years, so too we can expect the capitalists to bide their time. As predators, they will watch carefully and probe for any weakness. When they think the time is right, they will strike. That is the reason they have to be completely crushed, under the Dictatorship Of the Proletariat.

PART 10

GERMAN-SOVIET NON AGGRESSION PACT OF 1939 AND THE GREAT PATRIOTIC WAR

The whole world was shocked in 1939, at the time of the signing of the German-Soviet Non Aggression Pact. Each side agreed to not go to war with each other, for a period of ten years.

It was only natural that the capitalists would be shocked and horrified, as the imperialist powers were once again squabbling over a possible redivision of the world. Once again the Anglo-French alliance had visions of Russian soldiers being used as cannon fodder against the well entrenched German positions. They were graciously prepared to put aside their differences, to forget that they had made every effort to destroy the newly created Soviet Socialist Republic, in the interest of maintaining their colonies. In fact, they were quite fully prepared to fight, once again, the War To End All Wars, the Great War, the First World War. The Germans had other ideas.

Perhaps the Anglo-French imperialists had forgotten the old expression that "a man who has been flogged, is worth two who have not". Germany was the equivalent of the man who had been flogged. They had been beaten in that war, and had learned their lesson well. Even the imperialists are capable of learning!

In preparation for a resumption of trench warfare, the French imperialists had constructed a modern marvel, the equivalent of a "Great Wall". They actually had the hare brained idea that this would stop the German hordes in their tracks! In much the same way, Trump had the idea that the North American wall would stop the "thieves and drug smugglers", from Mexico and points south! No one ever accused the imperialists of being original! They are ever so predictable!

Yet as the German imperialists had been "once flogged", they were determined to avoid the mistakes of the previous war. That included becoming involved in trench warfare, as well as fighting a war on two fronts. With that in mind, they came up with the idea of blitzkrieg, or lightning warfare, in which aircraft, armour and artillery, working in unison, would punch holes through the enemy defences, through which infantry would pour.

Bear in mind that lightning warfare was dreamed up in the twentieth century. Now in the twenty first century, one hundred years later (almost), the American imperialists are supremely proud of themselves, as they have come up with the same idea. The only difference is that they have changed the name to that of "shock and awe". Yet they are still building their very own Maginot Line, along the southern border with Mexico. Old habits are so hard to break!

As for the previous mistake of war on two fronts, the German imperialists, the Nazis, had that covered too. They proposed the Non Aggression Pact with the Soviet Union, and of course, the Soviets welcomed this.

Contrary to popular belief, Stalin and the Soviets were not entirely stupid. They knew precisely the plan of the Nazis, led by Hitler. They had read his book, Mein Kampf. In that book, he made it clear that he regarded the territory to the east, which is to say the Soviet Union, as "living space" for the "superior" Aryan race. Those who were occupying that territory, the Slavs, he regarded as mere "subhumans".

In preparation for the upcoming war, the Soviets needed time. Since the November 7 revolution of 1917, they had worked a modern miracle. The war had left the country devastated, and was followed by a three year civil war. Yet in the following twenty years, they had managed to industrialize the country, to the level of the most modern of the so called "great powers". The trouble was that most of their industry was in the west of the country, well within reach of the German bombers. They needed time to move that industry, especially the heavy industry, across the Ural mountains, to the east. The Non Aggression Pact gave them the time, the two years, they so desperately needed.

As is well known, the Nazis broke the Non Aggression Pact on June 22, 1941, with the largest land based invasion in history. In fact, three million men took part in the initial attack. In the process, Hitler broke his own cardinal rule, that of not fighting a war on two fronts. After all, Germany was, at that time, still fighting a war with Britain.

As for those who find it strange that Hitler would break his own rule, it has been suggested that the man was insane, so such behaviour, on the part of an insane man, was not too surprising. To this I can only respond that such behaviour, on the part of any imperialist, is not too surprising. All imperialists are completely devoid of any sense of morality or principle. In much the same way, they are generally devoid of logic. They are merely convinced that they have the God given right to do anything they please. This is another way of saying that they are completely reactionary.

After Hitler got what he wanted, the Non Aggression Pact with the Soviet Union, he initiated his war of aggression with the other imperialist powers. The first country he invaded was Poland.

The bourgeois press, which is to say the capitalist press, has devoted a great deal of ink, to the so called "partition of Poland", between Nazi Germany and the Soviet Union. They maintain that the Nazis came to an agreement with the Soviets, to divide the country of Poland between them. They offer this as proof of "collaboration" between "two competing dictatorial regimes". The facts are quietly and calmly ignored.

The fact is that the country of Poland was one of the countries which was contained within the Russian empire. At the time of the socialist November 7 revolution of 1917, Poland and other republics, contained within the Russian empire, had achieved their independence. Then, after the end of the First World War, the imperialist countries armed and equipped those countries, including Poland, in an attempt to crush the Soviet Russian Republic. As I have previously documented this, there is no need to repeat it. This resulted in a war between Soviet Russia and Poland, which ended in a treaty which granted Poland the western Ukraine, and part of Byelorussia. In 1939, the Soviet Union declared that treaty null and void, and determined to reclaim that which was rightfully theirs. After all, the people who lived in those occupied territories were anxious to return to their independent republics. The Soviets did not invade Poland.

They merely occupied that which was properly part of the Soviet Union. It was Nazi Germany which occupied Poland.

As is well known, in 1939 and 1940, the Nazis invaded and occupied the countries of Poland, Czechoslovakia, Belgium and France. That which is not so well known is the fact that the Nazis then took over the factories of those countries, and put them to work building armoured vehicles, panzers. In the west, these armoured vehicles are commonly referred to as tanks, but as the word panzer is more accurate, I have chosen to use that word. As a result of this, at the time of the Nazi invasion, of the Soviet Union, on June 22, 1941, they had far more panzers than the Soviets.

Of course, the capitalist producers of documentaries claim that at the time of the invasion, the Soviets had "twenty thousand panzers, more than the armies of the rest of the world combined". It is safe to say that the capitalists have out done themselves. They have managed to sink to new depths of nonsense. To even suggest that an underdeveloped peasant country, after seven years of war, which left the country in ruins, could then industrialize to the extent that they could produce more armoured vehicles than the rest of the world combined, and within twenty years, no less! The individual who came up with that bit of idiocy deserves an award: Jackass of the Year!

Incidentally, at the time of the invasion of the Soviet Union, the Second World War was transformed. Up until that point, it was a war to once again, redivide the world. Once again, Germany wanted more colonies, and once again, the other imperialist powers were determined to keep their colonies. Further, once again, the working people of those countries were urged to transform the imperialist war into a revolutionary war, a just war, to overthrow their own bourgeois. All of that changed with the invasion of the one and only socialist country in the world.

At that point, the imperialist war changed into a just war, a war to defend the socialist Soviet Union.

To return to the invasion of the Soviet Union, by the Nazis, the overwhelming superiority of panzers was decisive, in that the Soviet Red Army was forced to retreat. They simply could not stand up to the assaults of the fast moving Nazi panzers. It was either retreat of be surrounded and annihilated.

The response of Stalin and the Soviet High Command, was to initiate an orderly retreat. They decided to sacrifice land, in return for time. They had a great abundance of land, and they could afford to lose a small part of it, in return for time.

As part of the orderly retreat, a scorched earth policy was enacted. All wooden buildings were burned. All metal buildings were blown up. All bridges were destroyed. All stocks of food and ammunition were either sent to the rear, or destroyed. All livestock was sent to the rear, or killed. All fields, which had been planted, were ploughed under. Anything the Nazis could have found to be useful, was destroyed. The order was to leave nothing to the Nazis, and for the most part, this order was carried out.

At the same time, eighty percent of the industry in the western part of the country, which is to say fifteen hundred huge factories, were dismantled and moved to the east, across the Ural mountains, and reassembled. In this way, they were not allowed to fall into the hands of the Nazis, and were also out of the range of enemy bombers. As soon as they were in place, in their new homes, production was immediately resumed. Of course this meant that at the beginning of the war, Soviet production took a nose dive. This was not immediately felt, as at the beginning of the war, the Soviets had a vast stock pile of equipment. After all, they had been preparing for the war for many years. It was only in the beginning of the following year, that the shortages made themselves felt.

The whole country mobilized for the war, The Great Patriotic War. It was not a war for socialism, of class against class, it was a war of survival. The Nazis made clear their determination to destroy the Soviet Union, to occupy all of European Russia, to kill most of their people, with the remainder to be used as slave labour. If nothing else, this provided the Soviets with a great motivation to resist the Nazi invaders.

Most of the men left the factories and joined the military. As military training was compulsory in the Soviet Union, so that almost all men had military training, it did not take long for fresh divisions to take shape. The women replaced them in the factories, as well as in the fields. They were determined that a woman could run a machine as well as any man. As well, they ran tractors, trains, busses, trucks and boats. The teen agers, too young for the military, also worked in the factories. The seniors came out of retirement and returned to work, without pay, as they had their pensions. Those who were rather feeble, worked the hours they could, perhaps in the cooking and cleaning. The senior women took part in raising the children. Everyone received military training of some sort. When necessary, all took part in digging trenches, as when the enemy panzers were too close.

As well, a great many women joined the Red Army, and not just as nurses and medics. They were not expected to join the infantry, as it was not reasonable to expect them to carry such heavy packs. Yet they joined the armour, as panzer commanders. They joined the artillery, as they could site in an artillery piece as well as any man. They became mechanics, as they could also pull a wrench as well as any man. Not only that, but they became pilots, of fighters and bombers. Some of them specialized in night bombing, as they had excellent eye sight.

The enemy soldiers had a particular hatred for these women pilots in their bombers, these "night witches", as after a hard day of fighting, a soldier wanted to sit down and relax, with a coffee and a smoke, perhaps beside a camp fire. Yet the glow from a cigarette was the very thing the pilots were able to spot, and they generally responded with a little gift.

Perhaps most surprising, to all but the ladies involved, was the fact that the women made such superb snipers. Of course, the basic requirement of a fine sniper is the ability to be supremely accurate. Yet perhaps more importantly, was the ability to be patient and observant. The lady snipers were famous for lying motionless, for hour after hour. The whole time they were watching the enemy troops through their scopes, mounted on their rifles. Numerous shots they would pass over, waiting for an officer to appear. Of course, the officers at the front never wore any sign of rank, and the enlisted men were not required to salute officers. Yet the ladies, from watching the behaviour of the troops, were able to determine that an officer had just made an appearance. At that point, they would shoot the officer. This they did consistently, and to great effect.

Whereas male snipers tended to be more concerned with their number of kills, the females focused on "quality", rather than quantity. They were of the opinion that it was far more effective to kill an officer, rather than an enlisted man. The high command of the opposing armies were also of that opinion. They had a particular hatred for the lady snipers.

Now the capitalist "documentaries" are unanimous, in their reports that the start of the war was disastrous for the Soviet Union. They maintain the Soviet High Command was caught completely off guard, Stalin suffered a "breakdown" of some sort, possibly stayed drunk for several days, the Red Army troops were consistently surrounded and surrendered in their tens of thousands, and by November, Moscow was threatened. They would have us believe that within the first five months of the war, the Red Army lost five million men. Then the Soviets counter attacked, across a front of eight hundred kilometres or five hundred miles, and pushed back the invading armies one hundred miles, or one hundred sixty kilometres. Duh!

At that time, the population of the Soviet Union was roughly the same as that of America. To imagine that an American army could sustain losses of five million men, within five months, and then counter attack, is utterly ridiculous. It is simply not possible.

In fact, as the Red Army retreated, certain detachments were left behind as a "rear guard". Their duty was to delay the invading troops, to hold them back for as long as possible, in order for the bulk of the Red Army to retreat "in good order", which is to say with their equipment. At the time the invading armies broke through this rear guard, then it was necessary for those troops to also retreat, and set up another line of defence.

As can be well imagined, this took a heavy toll on the rear guard troops. Many of them were killed in combat. Others found themselves surrounded, and while a few surrendered, many either fought to the death or escaped into the forests and swamps, there to join the civilian partisans.

Without doubt, the first few months of the war seemed to be a complete disaster, from the viewpoint of the common Red Army soldier, stationed at the front. Yet the fact remains that the bulk of the Red Army retreated in good order, complete with their equipment. The fact also remains that the advancing Nazi invaders took some heavy losses, breaking through the Soviet lines of defence. As well, faced with a "scorched earth", the supply lines became ever longer, as everything the army needed, had to be transported a very long distance. It did not help that the Russian "roads", existed mainly on paper. The Russian rail network, when captured intact, was of a different dimension than that of European rails, so that the German trains could not run on those tracks.

By November, the Nazi offensive, the blitzkrieg, or lightning war, had slowed down to a crawl. The fall rains had turned the roads into a sea of mud. The Germans were close to Moscow, but bogged down. Even so, the Soviet High Command decided to hold the November 7 military parade, within the capitol of Moscow, as a show of defiance to the Nazis and the world. Even though the capitol was threatened, this parade helped to boost morale within the Red Army.

The rest of the world could not believe that the Soviet Union could stand up to the Nazi assault. One major American magazine even announced that the Soviet Union was beaten, and explained that the country never had a chance, against the mighty Nazi juggernaut.

The Soviet High Command had been expecting the Japanese to attack from the east, and were prepared with a huge army. But the Japanese imperialists decided to wait until their Nazi allies crushed the Soviets, and then perhaps go on the offensive. Besides, they were more focused on their main enemy, America. Hence the attack on Pearl Harbour.

The Soviet spies in Japan informed Stalin of this, and he responded by sending thirty divisions, half a million men and all their equipment, towards Moscow. These were the Siberian troops, some of the finest troops in the country. They were accustomed to enduring great hardships, as well as the cold, and were well equipped for winter fighting.

By contrast, the invading troops had no winter equipment at all. The Nazis were accustomed to short campaigns, and expected the Soviet Union to collapse within a few weeks, two or three months, at worst. They made no preparations for a winter campaign.

As a result of this, in early December, the prayers of the invading troops were answered. The roads became quite firm, once again. In fact, they were frozen solid. The temperatures dropped to forty below zero, and men and equipment froze. The equipment was completely unprepared for the cold, as were the men. The engines would not start, and the oil froze so that the machine parts would not move. Hitler decided to postpone the destruction of the Soviet Union until the spring. The offensive was called off.

This severe cold was the very thing the Soviet High Command had been counting upon. It was every bit as predictable as the fall rains. At the same time as the invading troops were calling off their offensive, the Soviets ordered a counter attack. Across a five hundred mile front, or eight hundred kilometres, they attacked, and pushed back the invaders one hundred miles, or one hundred sixty kilometres. Welcome to the Great Patriotic War.

PART 11

STALINGRAD AND ORDER 227

In the spring of 1942, Hitler and the Nazi high command decided upon a different strategy. Instead of trying to destroy the Soviet Union at one stroke, they would instead deprive the country of the oil required to fuel the Red Army. As most of the oil came from the Caucasus, in the southern part of the country, it stood to reason to capture those oil fields. Then, acting upon impulse, Hitler also decided to capture the modern industrial city which was built upon the banks of the Volga, the city which bore the name of the man whom he hated, more than anyone else. That man was Stalin. The city was Stalingrad.

It should be noted that the Volga river was a main artery, within the Soviet Union. It may be compared to the American Mississippi River, in that countless boatloads of goods travel those rivers. In the case of the Soviet Union, most of the oil was barged from the oil fields, up the Volga, to various parts of the country. Without that oil, the Soviet war effort would be severely compromised. Both the oil fields of the Caucasus, and the Volga River, had to be secured.

Yet in the summer of 1942, there were "cowards and rumour mongers" who were busy spreading the seditious rumours that the Soviet Union was endless, that the retreat that had begun the previous summer could go on forever. Such people were only too happy to retreat, as a means of avoiding battle! It was with these people in mind that Stalin issued Order 227, commonly known as Not One Step Back!

"The enemy throws new forces to the front without regard to heavy losses and penetrates deep into the Soviet Union, seizing new territories, destroying our cities and villages, violating, plundering and killing the Soviet population . . . The German invaders penetrate towards Stalingrad, to Volga and want at any cost to trap Kuban and the northern Caucasus, with their oil and grain . . . The territory of the Soviet state is not a desert, but people—workers, peasants, intelligentsia, our fathers, mothers, wives, brothers, children . . . To retreat farther—means to waste ourselves and to waste, at the same time, our Motherland . . . therefore it is necessary to eliminate talk that we have the capacity endlessly to retreat . . . such talk is false and parasitic . . . this leads to the conclusion, it is time to finish retreating. Not one step back! Such should now be our main slogan . . . The Supreme General Head Quarters of the Red Army Commands:

"1)Military councils of the fronts and first of all front commanders should:

"a)Unconditionally eliminate retreat moods in the troops and with a firm hand bar propaganda that we can and should retreat further east

"b) form defensive squads, up to 200 persons each, and put them directly behind unstable divisions and require them in case of panic and scattered withdrawls of elements of the divisions to shoot in place panic mongers and cowards"

That is the gist of the order, and contains the clause, which so many people find to be so objectionable, that of the defensive squads, with orders to shoot cowards and panic mongers.

It is clear that the order was meant to boost morale within the Soviet Union. This was at a time when the country was at a cross roads. The previous order of retreat, given at the time of the invasion, was correct, as at that time the situation was different. Yet the retreat had stopped, at the gates of Moscow, and the Soviets had counter attacked. The summer of 1942 was not the time to retreat again, especially as to retreat beyond the Volga would have been a disaster. Hence the order Not One Step Back!

The order to shoot cowards and panic mongers was meant to be put into effect, only as an absolute last resort.

Of course the capitalist documentaries would have us believe that the Soviet Union had an unlimited amount of manpower. They did not, just as they did not have an unlimited number of panzers. They did have a great many common people, workers and peasants, who were determined to crush the Nazi invaders.

The capitalist press tends to ignore the fact that the Soviet Union was invaded by the countries of Germany, Austria, Italy, Czechoslovakia, Rumania, Hungary and Finland. The combined population of those countries was very likely even more than the "unlimited" population of the Soviet Union.

Recently a very popular movie was filmed, which is typical of the capitalist slander of the Soviet Union. In that movie, which is set in Stalingrad, we see the NKVD troops killing countless Red Army soldiers. We even see soldiers being sent into battle without rifles! That is absolute nonsense. It is ridiculous to even suggest that the mighty German Sixth army, which had marched across western Europe, was defeated by men who were charging machine guns, with their bare hands!

In fact, it is reported that the Sixth Army, with a total of twenty two German divisions, 330,000 men, were ordered to capture the city of Stalingrad. In addition, their flanks were protected by over half a million of their allies, Hungarian, Rumanian and Italian troops. In the summer of 1942, Hitler ordered his generals to capture the city at all costs, and the Soviet High Command ordered their generals to hold the city, at all costs. The unstoppable force met the immovable object!

The Soviet High Command recognized that Hitler was infatuated with the city, determined to capture it, and decided to use this to their advantage. The city itself became the bait in a huge trap. The troops inside the city were sent just enough reinforcements and equipment to keep the city from falling into the hands of the Germans. At the same time, vast amounts of troops and equipment were gathered, far to the north and far to the south of the city.

The Soviets also recognized that the weak link in the chain was in the troops who were defending the flanks. While the German troops were highly trained and well equipped, their allies, who were defending the flanks, tended to be somewhat less so. With that in mind, the plan was to attack the weak flanks, with overpowering armour, artillery and air power, establish a break through into which the infantry would pour, and encircle the entire Sixth Army. In other words, use the tactics of blitzkrieg, which the Nazis had used so well against the powers of western Europe, and to use it against the Nazis.

In late November, Hitler gave a speech in which he declared that the battle of Stalingrad was all but over. Merely a few "small pockets of resistance" had to be mopped up. The Soviets had other ideas. They attacked the flanks, far to the north and the south, broke through the defences and circled far to the west. Four days later, the two arms of the pincers met, far to the rear of the Sixth Army. This army, as well as possibly half a million of their allies, found themselves in a huge "kessel", a cauldron, surrounded by determined Soviet troops.

Much has been written concerning the resistance of the surrounded German Sixth army. Almost nothing has been written concerning the fact that half a million Hungarian, Rumanian and Italian troops were also surrounded. It is generally acknowledged that they gave way almost immediately, after they were attacked. After all, their hearts were not into it. They had no stomach for the war. It is very likely that they also surrendered, almost immediately. The history books have written volumes concerning the resistance of the German troops, within the cauldron, but nothing concerning their allies.

The Soviet High Command expected Hitler to issue his usual order to "stand fast", and in fact they were likely counting on this. He assured the commanders of the Sixth Army that the army would be supplied by air, and that a relief column was on the way. He lied.

For the following three months, the Soviets tightened their grip on the cauldron, squeezing it ever tighter. German attempts to supply the Sixth Army by air, were large ineffective. A panzer relief column was unable to break through. At the end of January, the remnants of the Sixth Army surrendered. It was the turning point of the war.

PART 12

STALIN AND THE GULAGS

The capitalist press has also made a great commotion over the fact that Soviet prisoners were sent to Gulags, work camps located mainly in the north of the country. Apparently all the Russian prisons, which had been filled to overflowing, before the revolution, were shut down. The inmates were then forced to perform useful, manual labour. The capitalists would have us believe that this was a terrible thing!

It is safe to say that such a thing could never happen in America, after the revolution, if only because there are no prisons in America. There is no shortage of "correctional institutions", which the capitalists have graciously established, in lieu of prisons. Their main concern is with the health and well being of the misguided members of society, those who have been led astray. These thieves and killers, rapists and child molesters, drunks and dope addicts, are fed and clothed, sheltered and educated, and provided with councillors who explain to them the error of their ways. In time, they emerge from these facilities "corrected", prepared to take their place in society, as useful, productive citizens. Ha!

In fact, the capitalists, ever on the look out for a chance to make a buck, saw an opportunity right in front of them, in the form of the countless prisons in the country. It was simply a matter of having the government sign those prisons over to the corporations, changing their name to that of "correctional institutions", and then having the tax payer foot the bill for housing these "delinquent" members of society. Naturally, the more inmates, and the longer they stay locked up, the higher the profit.

This stands in stark contrast to the dastardly Communists, who closed down the Russian prisons and had the audacity to send such misguided members of society to "gulags", in which they were put to work! The nerve of some people! The very idea of forcing those who have never done an honest days work, to dig trenches, tunnels, and ditches! Such manual labour is completely beneath their dignity! Yet they were also forced to lay tracks for railroads, construct dams and bridges, clear land for power lines. They were forced to take part in building the country! The people who spent years in school, working hard—or at least paying a great deal—for an advanced degree, had no interest of swinging a shovel! Yet those who did not work, were not fed! The announcers, of the documentaries, even state—to their horror— that some people even died, performing that kind of work!

After the approaching American socialist revolution, under the Dictatorship Of the Proletariat, we can expect the "correctional institutions" to also be shut down. Those who belong in prison will soon be taking part in rebuilding the country, the same country the capitalists have done their best to destroy. They too will soon be building the railroads, dams, bridges and trenches. The technical term for this is infrastructure, and it is in a sad state of disrepair. They can also assist in cleaning up the environment. Who better to pick up garbage?

Then again, those who specialize in assaulting women, seniors, crippled and children, the helpless, will largely be exempt from this sort of labour. They will face their victims, and regardless of the outcome of that encounter, will never again be given the opportunity to indulge in that sort of behaviour. They may be given the opportunity to redeem themselves in other ways, perhaps working in under ground mines, perhaps in the Arctic. In that way, we will make sure that they never sneak away, and return to their old habits.

The documentaries do their best to slander Stalin, accusing him of owning a fleet of luxury vehicles and expensive houses, across the country. They also show him planting fruit trees, as a hobby, in his spare time. As if this is a terrible thing! They also show the Moscow subway, built with the workers in mind. It resembles a museum! It is well lit, spotless, with designs on the flooring and marble columns. What is wrong with that?

They even brought up the fact that the son of Stalin was serving as a lieutenant in the Red Army, and was captured, early in the war. Then at the time the Soviets captured a German Field Marshall, at Stalingrad, the Nazis offered to exchange this son of Stalin, this lieutenant, for the Field Marshall. Yet Stalin said no! Rather than giving credit to Stalin for standing on principle, they accuse him of being a terrible father.

Stalin died in 1953, and the capitalists were able to return to power, at least temporarily. Yet the legacy of Lenin and Stalin, in the form of the first socialist republic, the first Dictatorship Of the Proletariat, will live forever. Soon we will have the opportunity to carry on, in their footsteps.

PART 13

THE IMPENDING REVOLUTION

The current situation in America is quite similar to the situation of Russia, in the summer of 1917, in the period between the two revolutions. The first revolution overthrew the Czar, so that the common people had some democratic rights, at least on paper. Yet the war continued, and the people were still suffering terribly, hungry and cold. Now in America we also have unemployment, hunger, the virus, wide spread homelessness and gun violence. The word desperate comes to mind.

Strangely enough, the press is once again focused on Trump, if for no other reason than that he is determined to regain power, to once again be president. He is comparing the federal election to a "jewelry heist", in that the recovered jewels must be returned to their rightful owner. Of course he is referring to himself, as the true president, who was robbed of the election, and should be returned to power.

Working people watch the news, and are paying attention. By no means all of them are convinced that socialism, in the form of the Dictatorship Of the Proletariat, is the solution. Out of respect for those people, perhaps it is best to clarify the situation.

Many people may be confused with all this talk of a "grand jury". In fact, America is one of the few countries to still use a grand jury, apparently a hold over from British common law. Remarkably enough, it has exceptional power. Criminals fear this organization, with good reason. This calls for a little explanation.

The word grand means large, so that a grand jury is usually composed of twenty three people, as opposed to a regular jury of twelve. The members of this grand jury are chosen at random, and they tend not to be screened before hand. Only a federal or state prosecutor is involved, no judge or defence attorney. All concerned are sworn to secrecy, so that those being investigated may not even be aware of this, until being served an indictment. As for those who are not Philadelphia lawyers, an indictment just means to be charged with a crime.

The latest grand jury to be summoned, by the state of New York, will determine if Trump, as well as the Trump Organization, his adult children and closest associates, will face criminal charges. The plan is for the grand jury to meet three days a week, for six months, possibly longer. Further, this is classified as a "special" grand jury, in that "organized crime" could be involved. The implication is that the prosecutor wants Trump, his family and friends, to be treated as members of a crime network. If the grand jury agrees, then all could be charged with "racketeering", a very serious crime. The term RICO could even be thrown about, as it stands for Racketeering Influenced and Corrupt Organization. It was that sort of charge that bought down the "Teflon Don", John Gotti.

Under grand jury proceedings, the prosecutor presents the evidence that a crime has been committed. If a majority of the members, which is twelve, believe that there is "probable cause" to believe that a crime has been committed, then they can issue an "indictment", which is to say a charge of a crime. The grand jury can compel a witness to testify. That same witness has immunity from prosecution. The accused has no right to consult a lawyer or present a defence or to cross examine witnesses. They may not even be aware that they are being investigated!

No wonder the criminals are afraid of a grand jury! A simple majority is all that is required to issue charges, and "probable cause" is a far cry from "beyond a reasonable doubt"!

In this particular case, a District Attorney for the state of New York is the only one who gets to speak to the grand jury. It is reported that he is pushing for charges of tax evasion, witness tampering, money laundering and obstruction of justice, among other things. Those "other things" include a long list of possible charges, and are not limited to Trump. Other individuals may include his adult children, former personal lawyer, as well as his long time Chief Financial Officer, CFO. Further, that particular CFO may be facing the prospect of having his children also charged. It is reported that he has already hired his own lawyer, hopefully a good one. He is going to need it!

This CFO has worked for Trump most of his adult life, and it is impossible to "shovel coal" without getting dirty. He is looking at spending his "golden years" behind bars, in a "correctional facility", unless he "plays ball" with the prosecutor, in that he becomes a "cooperating witness". The mobsters call this "turning rat". All are agreed that he knows where "all the bodies are buried". He is going to need a good lawyer, an expensive lawyer, as there are no good, cheap lawyers.

The former personal lawyer for Trump is acting as an unofficial consultant to that particular CFO, as well as to another former lawyer for Trump, who is also the former mayor of New York City. This fellow is generously giving free advice, as "one good turn deserves another". He is of the opinion that Trump "threw him under the bus", after he performed years of faithful service. His advice, to these associates of Trump, is quite simple: Turn on Trump before he turns on you!

It is thought that a great many people would be well advised to heed this advice, as it is well known that Trump has the moral fibre of a mad dog. Yet most prosecutors are not terribly greedy, as they are usually content to have merely one person testify against the accused they are focused on, in this case, Trump. As all of his adult children and friends are being investigated, it is very likely that the first person to "turn rat" will be able to walk away, while the others may be facing some serious jail time. The speculation is that his daughter, as the smartest of his offspring (which is not saying much), will be the one to "sing like a canary", and get the best deal.

No doubt there are a great many people who scoff, at the idea of a billionaire being sent to prison! It is common knowledge that the rich people are able to hire the finest, most expensive lawyers—there are no fine, cheap lawyers—and those lawyers are able to keep their clients out of jail. True enough! Yet due to the revolutionary motion that is sweeping the country, his brethren, by which I mean the other members of his class, the bourgeoisie, his fellow billionaires, have decided that Trump is a "loose cannon", and has to go. Trump is on his way out. It is just a question of how many people he takes down with him.

Perhaps the capitalists are of the opinion, that by having the press focus on Trump, the revolutionary motion can be diverted onto some harmless path of social reform. Yet the journalists, especially the females, are expressing a sense of despair. They are reporting that gun violence, senseless shooting in America, is at an "epidemic level".

After a recent shooting in California, in which nine people were murdered, the governor of that state expressed his frustration and bewilderment. As he expressed the sentiment of the people of the country, I have decided to reproduce it here:

> "What the hell is wrong with us? What the hell is going on in the United States of America? There is a numbness, a sameness to this, and I think that is something we are all feeling. We are experiencing something not experienced anywhere else in the world. When are we going to come to grips with this?"

To think that the governor of California, of all people, would express the sentiments of the vast majority of Americans! But since you asked, dear governor, the answer to your question is that a revolution is brewing. All Americans will "come to grips" with this gun violence, this senseless killing, at the time of the revolution. That revolution is fast approaching.

Now is the time to get organized, in preparation for the revolution. It may help to think of this as a period of transition, from the time in which many working people still have faith in the two party system, to a time of realization that a socialist revolution is required.

At the time of the insurrection, we had best be ready. In Russia, 1917, people formed Soviets, which means Councils. Now in America, workers are forming Autonomous Zones. More such Zones must be created, across the country. The slogan of the day must be *proletarian organization!*

This is not to say that whole cities, or even parts of cities should be occupied, and declared Autonomous Zones. Far from it. Experience of the Seattle Autonomous Zone, as well as the Occupy Movement of several years ago, has shown that such occupations are invariably met with an attack, by an overwhelming force.

Capitalism is in a state of crisis. The ruling class, the billionaires, the bourgeoisie, are in a state of deadlock. The two mainstream political parties, both of which serve the capitalists, are "at each others throats". In the capital of Washington, they are quite evenly matched, so that neither party is able to pass any bills of consequence. The journalists, in a rare twist of humour, refer to this as "mutual assured obstruction".

Under a similar situation, in April of 1917, Lenin called for "a *real* class and revolutionary force, a proletarian militia that will *enjoy the confidence of all* the poor stratum of the population . . . and will *help them to organize,* help *them* to fight for bread, peace and freedom". (italics by Lenin)

It is not just the gun violence, the senseless acts of murder, that is rocking the nation. Ever more instances of racial discrimination, especially in the form of police brutality, are coming to the fore. The call for "police reform" is growing, for "defunding the police", to spend more money on social programs, less money on the police.

Now the mass murder of black people, in that possibly three hundred people were killed by a "mob", one hundred years ago, is making headlines. Biden has responded by proposing to invest more money in businesses which are "black owned". That is one sure way to inflame racial tensions!

The suggestion that the present government could be overthrown, in a revolution, may sound "far fetched", yet "in revolutionary times the limits of what is possible expand a thousand fold", according to Lenin. As we are living in "revolutionary times", we had best be prepared. The revolution will happen, when it happens. No revolution is "ready made". It is not about to wait for us. As that is the case, the question that comes immediately to mind is, then what?

In that case, the only way to *maintain power is to counter* the fine organization of the American capitalists, the billionaires, the bourgeoisie, with an equally fine *organization of the proletariat*!

I say that the organization of the capitalists is fine, because they have had a couple hundred years to perfect it! We have got to create an equally fine organization of the working class, the proletariat, and we have to create that immediately!

The workers, guided by their class instinct, have already begun to create this organization, in the form of Autonomous Zones. This is the nucleus of a new state apparatus, one which will be used to crush the capitalists, after the revolution. As the billionaires will be desperate to restore their "paradise lost", it will be necessary to suppress them. This calls for a *"peoples* militia", one which "consists of the *entire* population, of all adult citizens of *both* sexes, one that combines the functions of a people's army with police functions". (italics by Lenin)

Now is the time to train and arm "all adult citizens of both sexes", as members of a "peoples militia". As the revolution is being led by women, it is even more urgent to ensure that all women learn to handle firearms.

The members of each Zone will have to get their hands on helmets, gloves, shields, batons, bullet proof vests, tasers, paint balls and slings, along with a good supply of marbles, as ammunition for the slings. Detachments must be formed and workers must practice using these items. The paint balls can be used against the riot squad and their face visors. The slings can be used against the horses which will be sent against the workers. The idea is not so much to kill the horse, as to give the rider flying lessons. As well, each detachment should have several pipe wrenches, to be used to open the water hydrants. In that way, the water pressure will drop and the police will be deprived of one of their main weapons, the water cannons. Different members should be assigned different tasks.

Firearms and ammunition must also be stockpiled. The members of each Zone must get together and practice, with the various weapons. Try standing in formation and locking shields, striking and thrusting with the batons. Become familiar with the paint balls. Fire off a great many marbles, as in a short time, people can become quite accurate with these projectiles. Some people may prefer the hand held type, while others may favour the slings that revolve. Personal preference. The workers who have military training will prove to be most valuable in this training.

As well, personal preference applies to the use of firearms. At the risk of being accused of being a male chauvinist—which I am—allow me to point out that, as previously mentioned, the women are leading the American revolution. Yet many women are not terribly familiar with firearms, so that it is up to the men, especially the people with military training, to acquaint you ladies with those tools. I deliberately use the word tools, because that is precisely what they are. Just as a hammer or an axe is a tool, so too a firearm is a tool. All women should learn to use these tools. That tool does not have to be a cannon, in order to be effective. Bear in mind that the American army standard issue rifle, the M16, is twenty two calibre. It works just fine.

All members of each Zone must become familiar with the use of firearms! At the time of the Insurrection, two or three days will be critical. Key areas must be captured and held at all cost. Show the imperialists what it means to *fight like a girl!*

Prepare to build upon your revolutionary history. American children grow up, listening to stories of the Minutemen, and The Midnight Ride of Paul Revere, with the call, "To arms, to arms!" Take to heart the Declaration of Independence, in that your revolutionary forefathers gave you the right to "abolish any government which does not represent you". Follow in the footsteps of your ancestors. Pick up the torch of revolution. Be an inspiration for your children, just as your ancestors were an inspiration to you.

When next the call comes "To arms, to arms!", it will not be local, but national. Make sure your Zone is prepared to occupy and defend key points, at all costs. These may be communications centres, or highways, or bridges, train stations or airports. Be prepared. Be resolute. Be audacious. Be Revolutionary. Let the slogan be:

Victory or Death!

MORE IN
GERALD MCISAAC SCIENCE PROJECT

Republican Party Disintegrating

At the time of this writing, it is reported that at least 570,000 Americans have died, as a result of the Covid virus. That is the official death toll, while the unofficial death toll is estimated to be much higher. As well, the unemployment rate is at levels not seen since the great depression, although the official rate is much lower. But then, after people are out of work for a specified period of time, they are no longer classified as unemployed! Just think, if the capitalist quit counting the people out of work, the unemployment rate drops to zero! The combination of the virus, as people refer to it, and massive unemployment, is being spoken of as the twin crises in capitalism. Not that the capitalists are terribly concerned, as the stock market is soaring. It is breaking records, almost on a daily basis! The profits have never been higher! The billionaires, the super rich, the bourgeoisie, have never been more wealthy! Money just keeps pouring in! Who cares about the lowlifes who are whining about being hungry? As the queen of France once joked, if the common people have no bread, let them eat cake! On the other hand, the suffering of the vast majority of people has reached tremendous proportions. Hunger is widespread, with the food banks running out of food. Ever more people are homeless, forced to live on the streets. The more "fortunate" are able to find shelter in a vehicle. Others are sleeping under bridges. Very few have medical insurance, therefore no medical coverage. Healthy or not, they are on their own.

Women and Revolution

As I write this, President Biden has been in office for over one hundred days, the usual "honeymoon" period for any new president. He is proposing to spend money on a scale which is unprecedented. The opposition to this spending is intense, not because of the expense, but because it is not going to the military. Over half the money is earmarked for infrastructure, building and repairing roads, bridges, tunnels and such. The remainder is for social programs, involving students, workers and families. The plan to pay for these huge expenses is by raising taxes on the capitalists, the billionaires and their corporations. Although deeply opposed to these tax increases, the capitalists, the bourgeois, are deeply divided. In particular, the Republican Party is in a shambles. Most of the citizens who identify themselves as Republicans are convinced that the "election was stolen", that Trump was "robbed", that he really won the election, that he is the true president. They are quite vocal, determined to prove their case. The press is reporting that the "party infighting has reached a fever pitch". They are also of the opinion that the GOP, Republican Party, is having an "identity crisis", what ever that is! Even a former Republican president has weighed in on the subject. As he phrased it, in terms which are something less than eloquent, "it looks like we want to be extinct". Possibly he was referring to the Party, or possibly he was referring to his class, the bourgeoisie. Possibly he is so stunned, even he does not know what he is saying!